AF598796

A Keepsake

BALTIMORE

Antelo Devereux Jr.

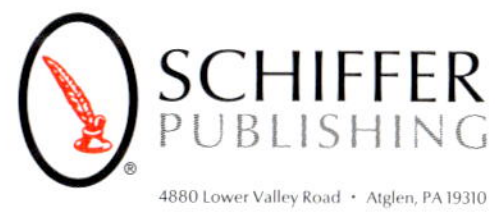

4880 Lower Valley Road • Atglen, PA 19310

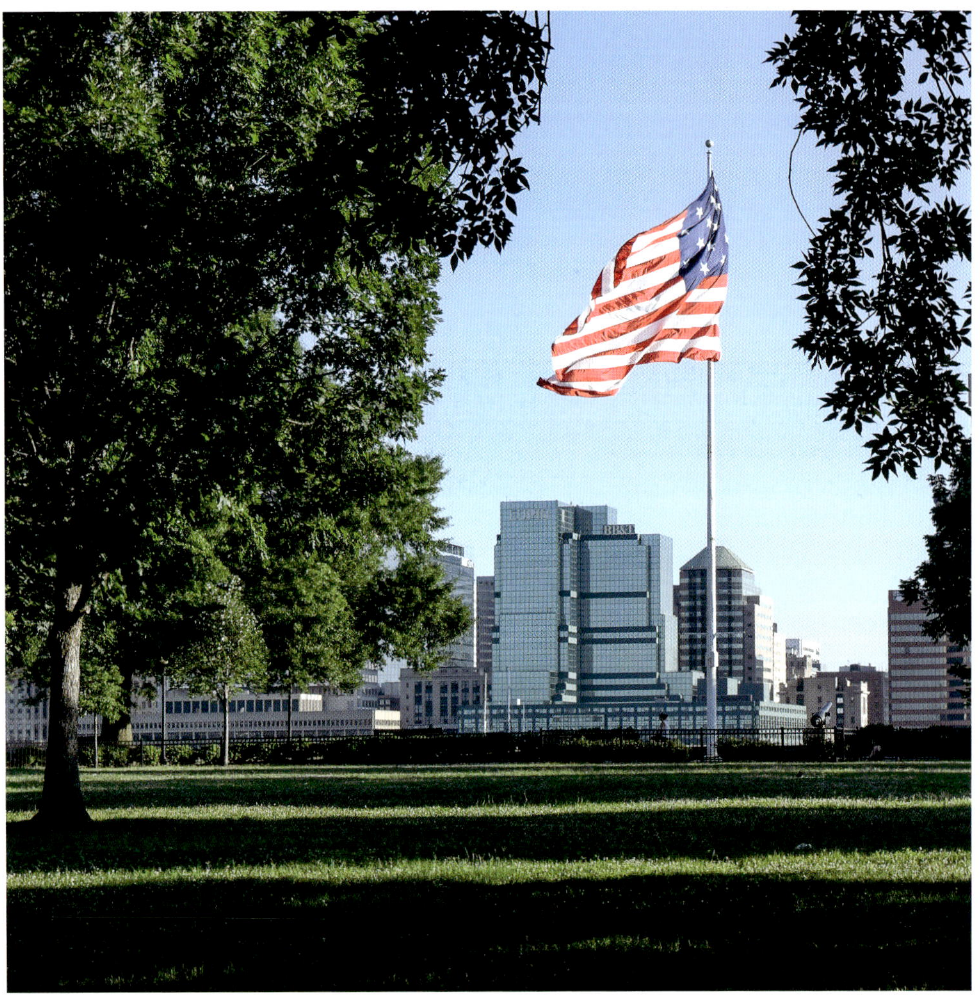

Federal Hill

INTRODUCTION

Named after the Calvert family manor in Ireland, the Port of Baltimore was created by the Maryland General Assembly for tobacco trade in 1706 at what is now Locust Point. Shortly thereafter, in 1729, the Town of Baltimore was established just west of Jones Falls.

Baltimore's location on the Patapsco River afforded excellent shipping access and a site for a fort to protect the entrance to the port. Fort McHenry would prove its worth in 1814, when the British attacked to no avail after burning the US Capitol. The nightlong battle not only stymied the British but pretty much finalized the result of the Revolutionary War and inspired Francis Scott Key to write what became the National Anthem.

Thanks to the Baltimore and Ohio Railroad, Baltimore's harbor grew to be an active, viable shipping center and second-largest port in the country. More recently the city has converted its Inner Harbor into a major tourist attraction and commercial center. Redevelopment has radiated from Harbor Place to include the National Aquarium, hotels, Fells Point, museums, housing, a convention center and Oriole Park at Camden Yards to the west.

Baltimore is a northern city with southern welcoming grace, charm, and culture. It is a vibrant place replete with commerce, museums, and historic sights, and people on the streets seem pleased to greet a passerby with a hello or good morning. Why not? Deciding which of many images to include in this book hasn't been easy, because the city is rich with historic sights and visual opportunities. I believe the following 90 photographs will convey that to the viewer.

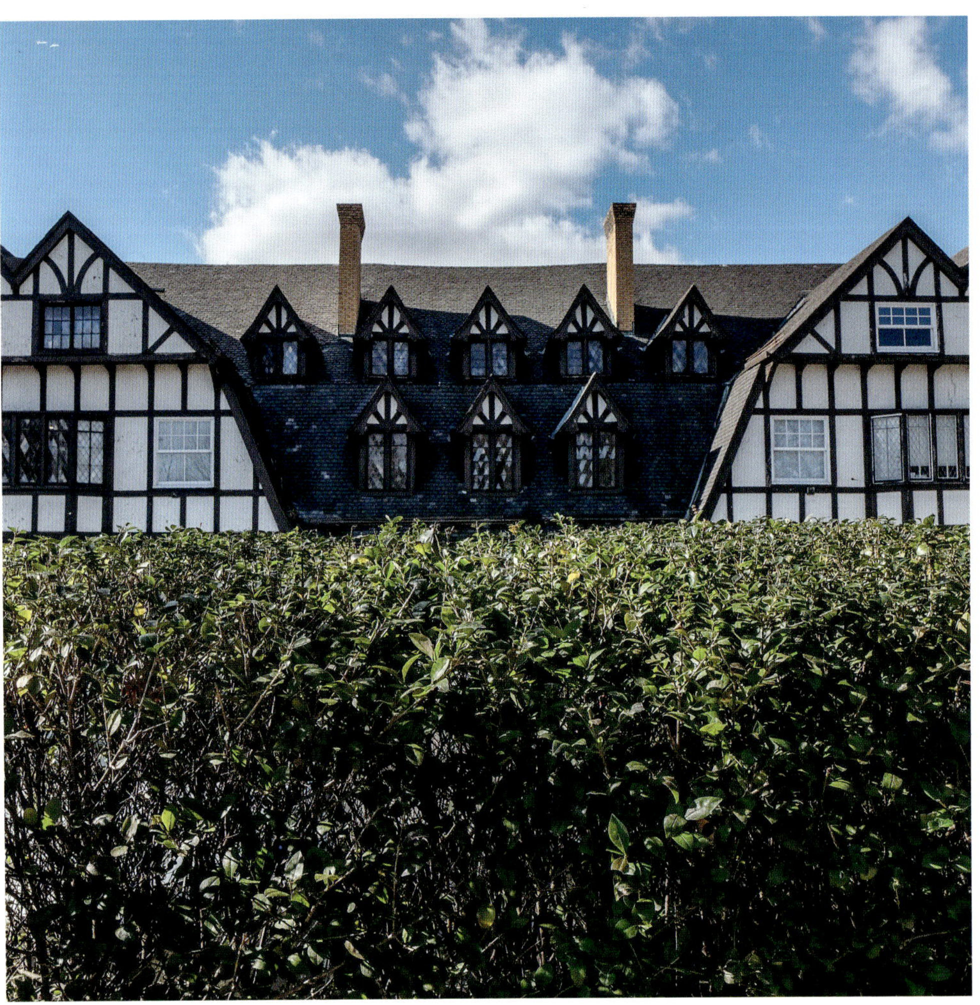

First strip mall, Rowland Park

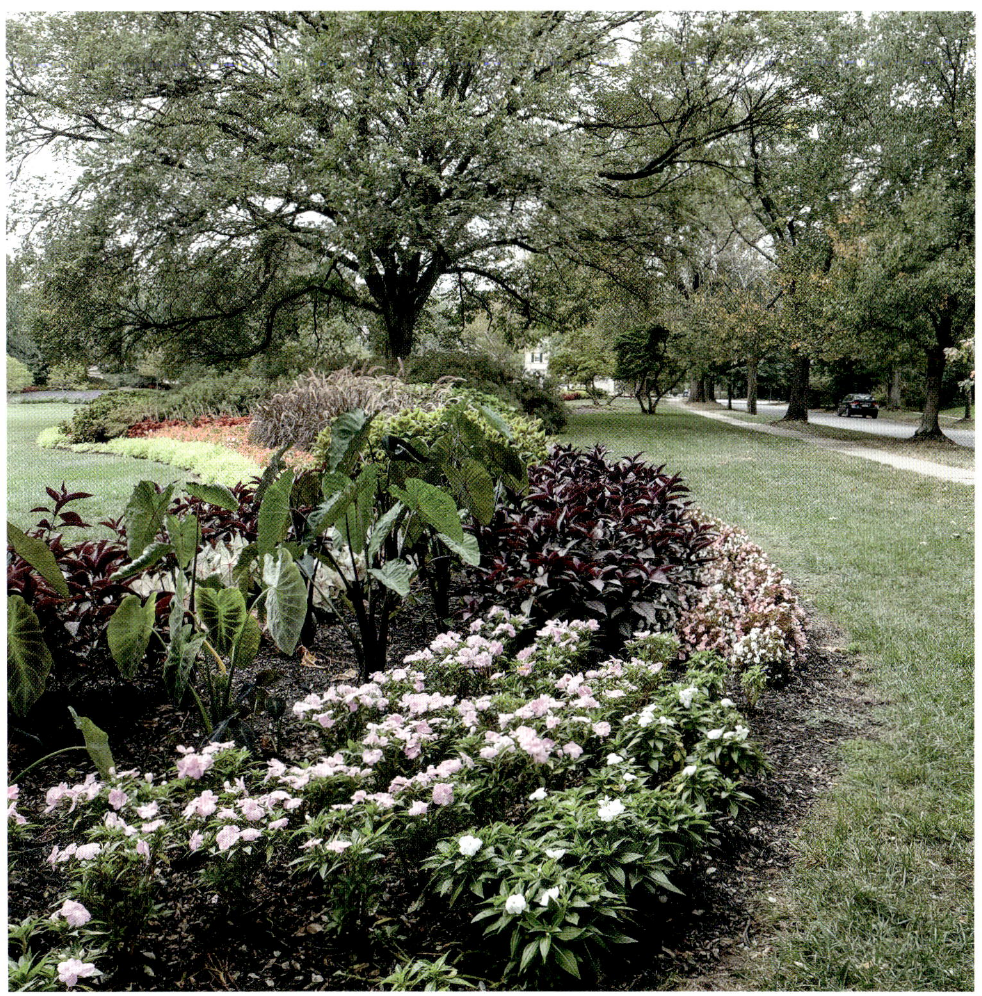

Sherwood Gardens, Guilford

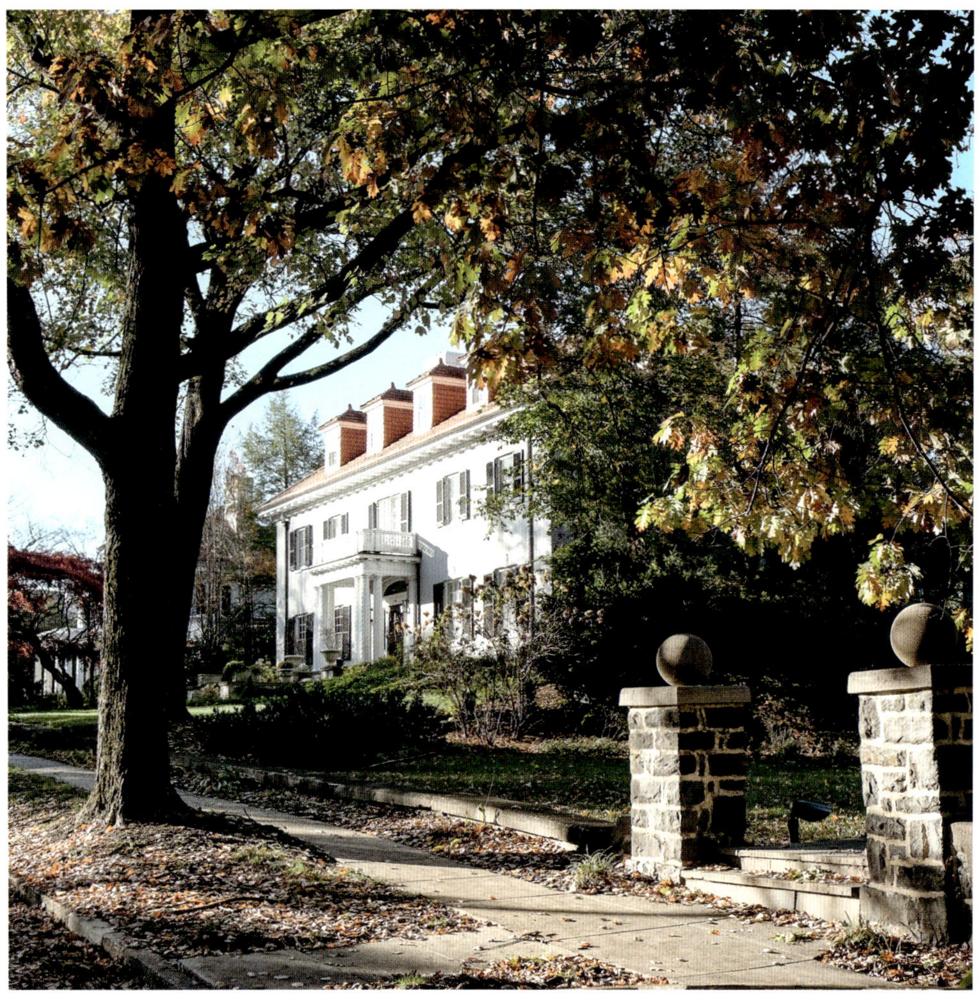

Rowland Park

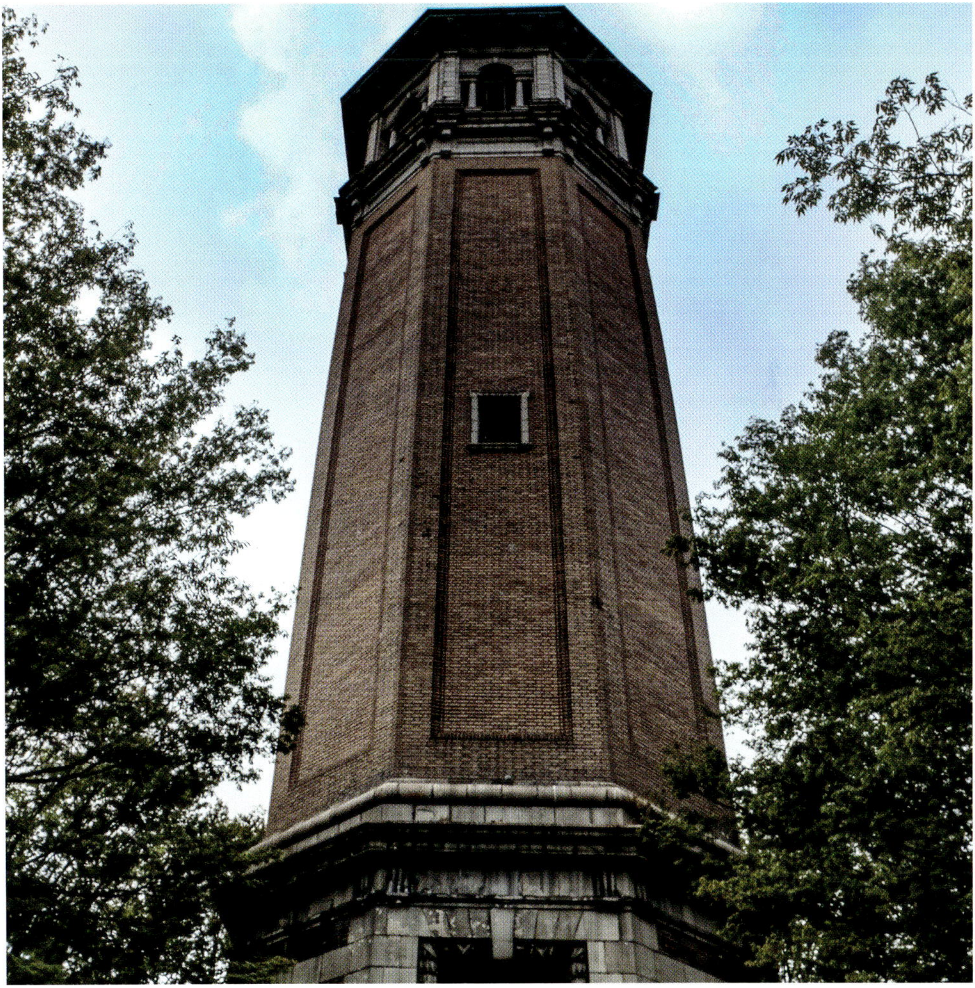

Rowland Park Water Tower

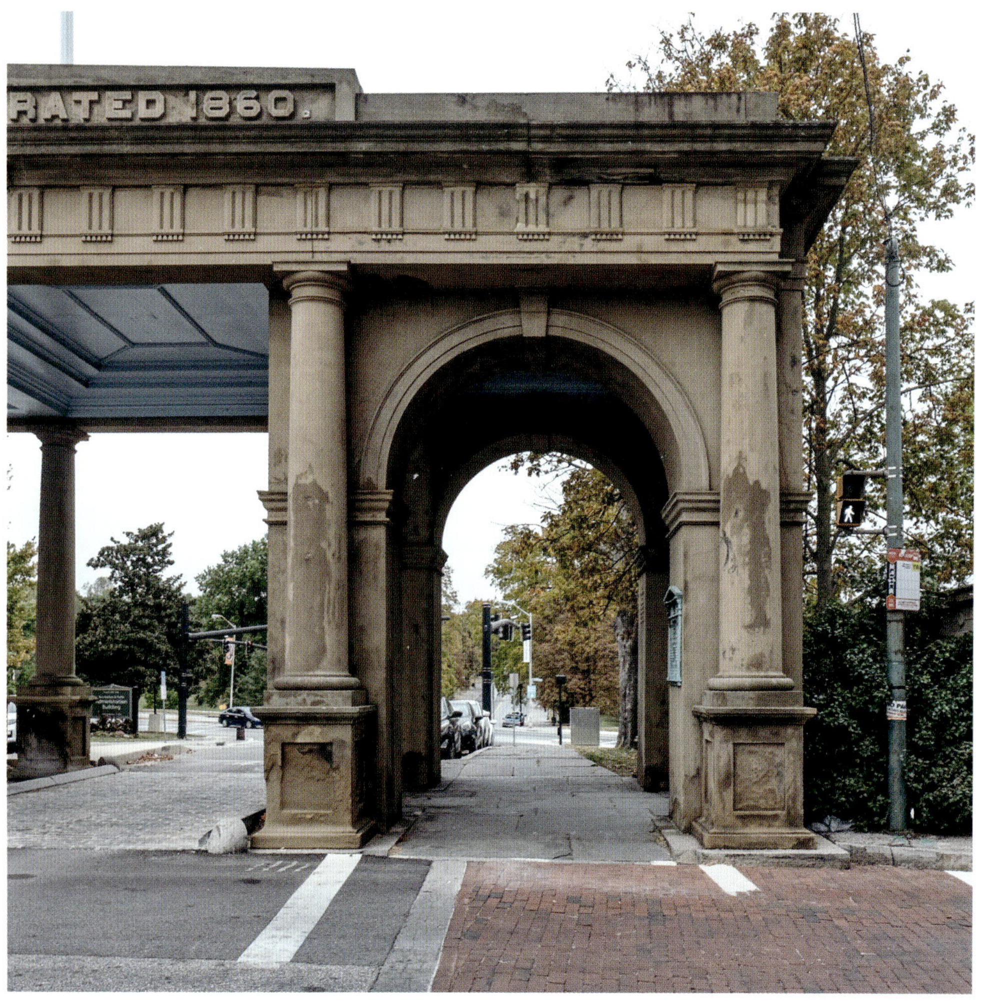

Druid Hill

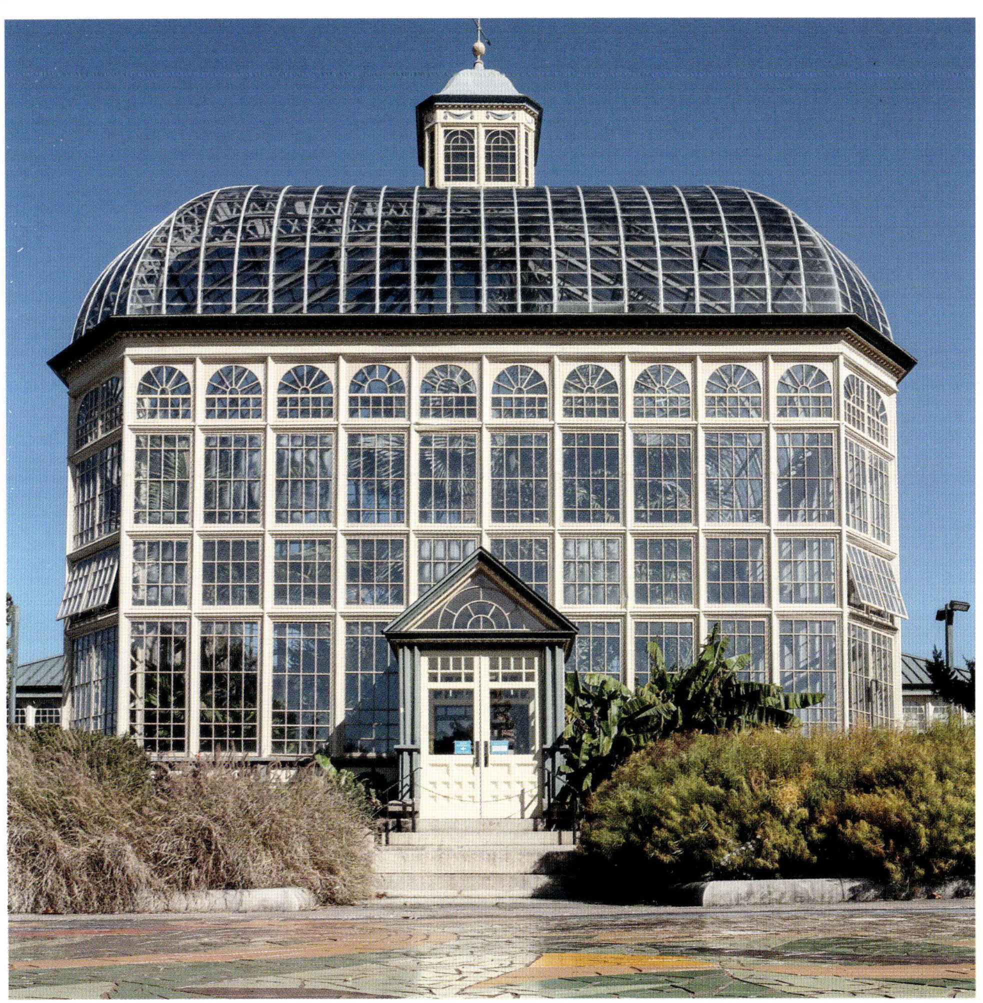

Rawlings Conservatory, Druid Hill Park

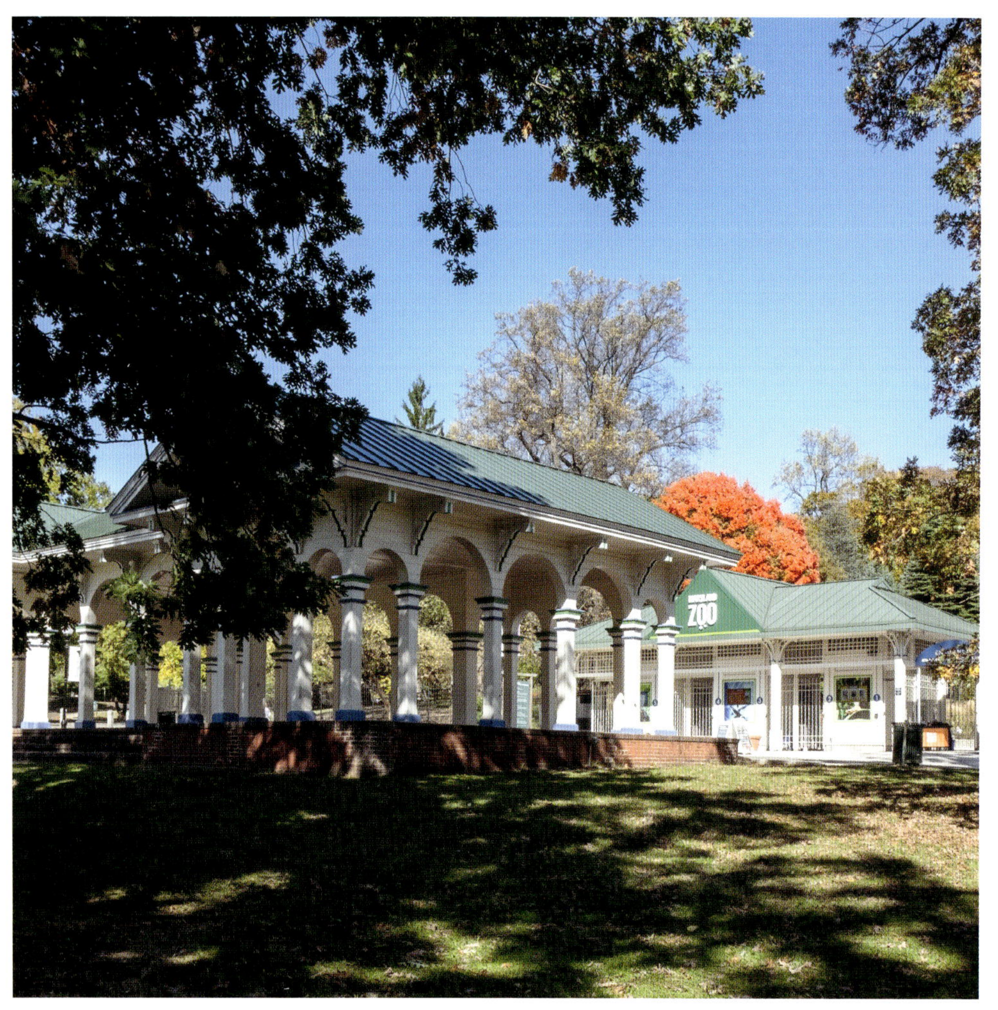

Maryland Zoo, Druid Hill Park

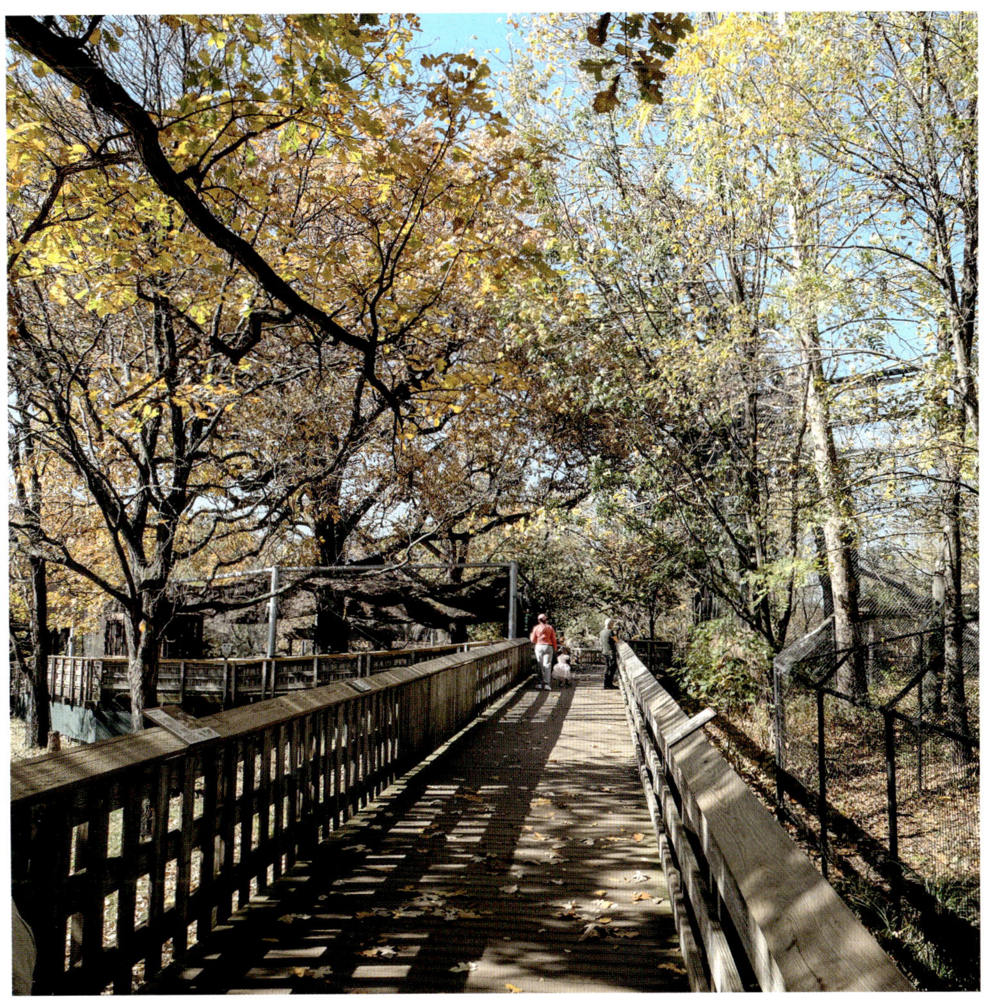

Maryland Zoo, Druid Hill Park

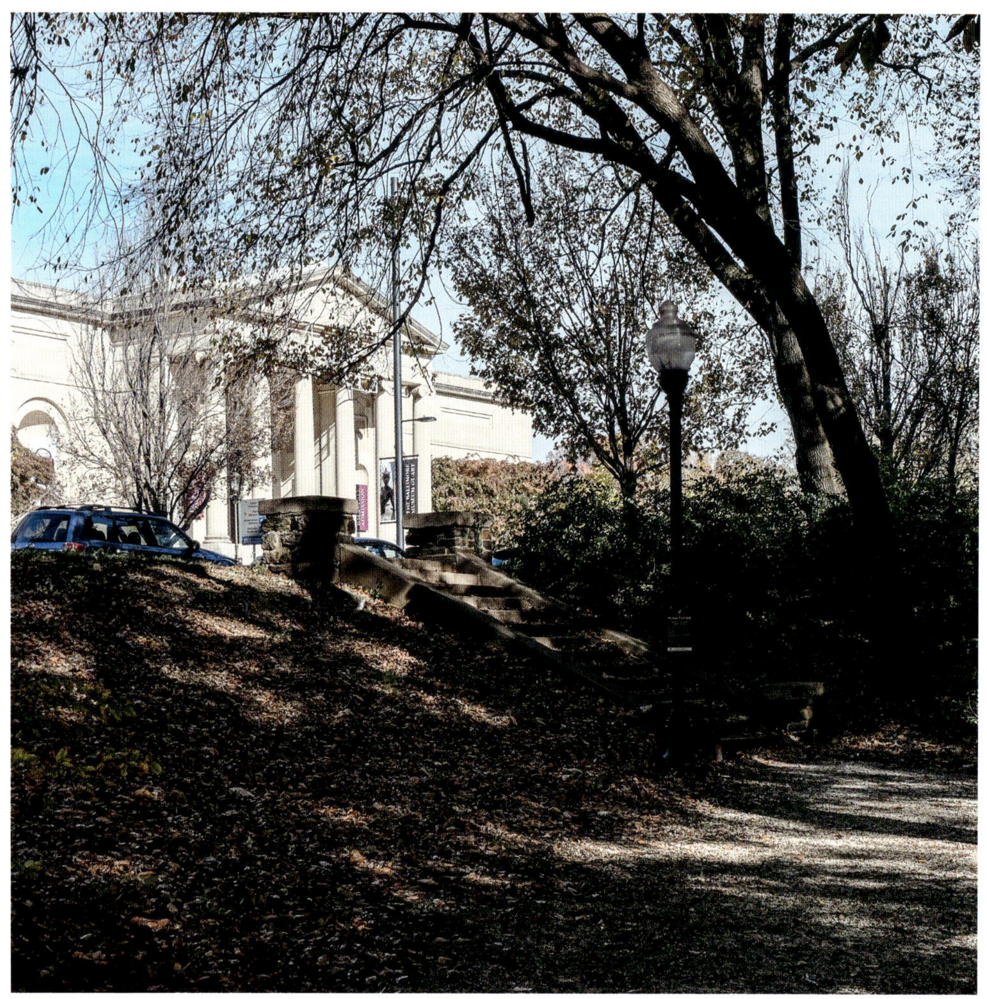

Baltimore Museum of Art

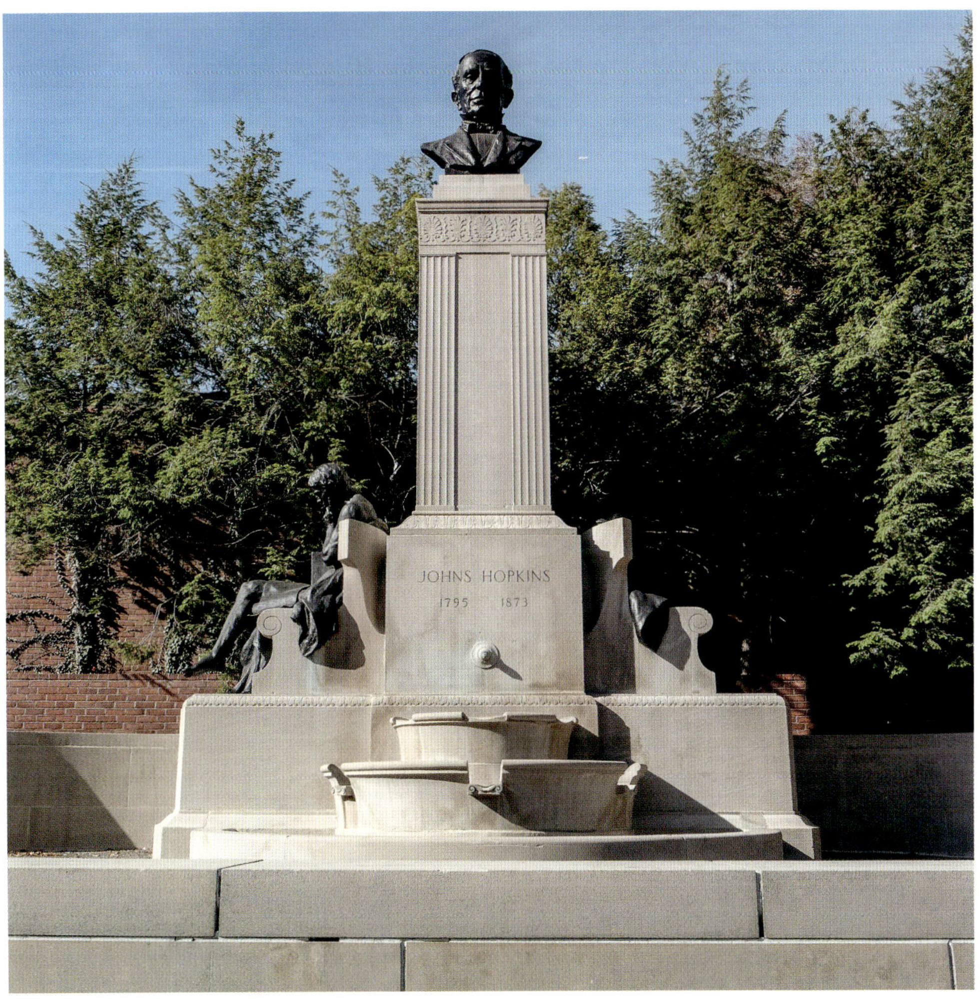

Johns Hopkins University

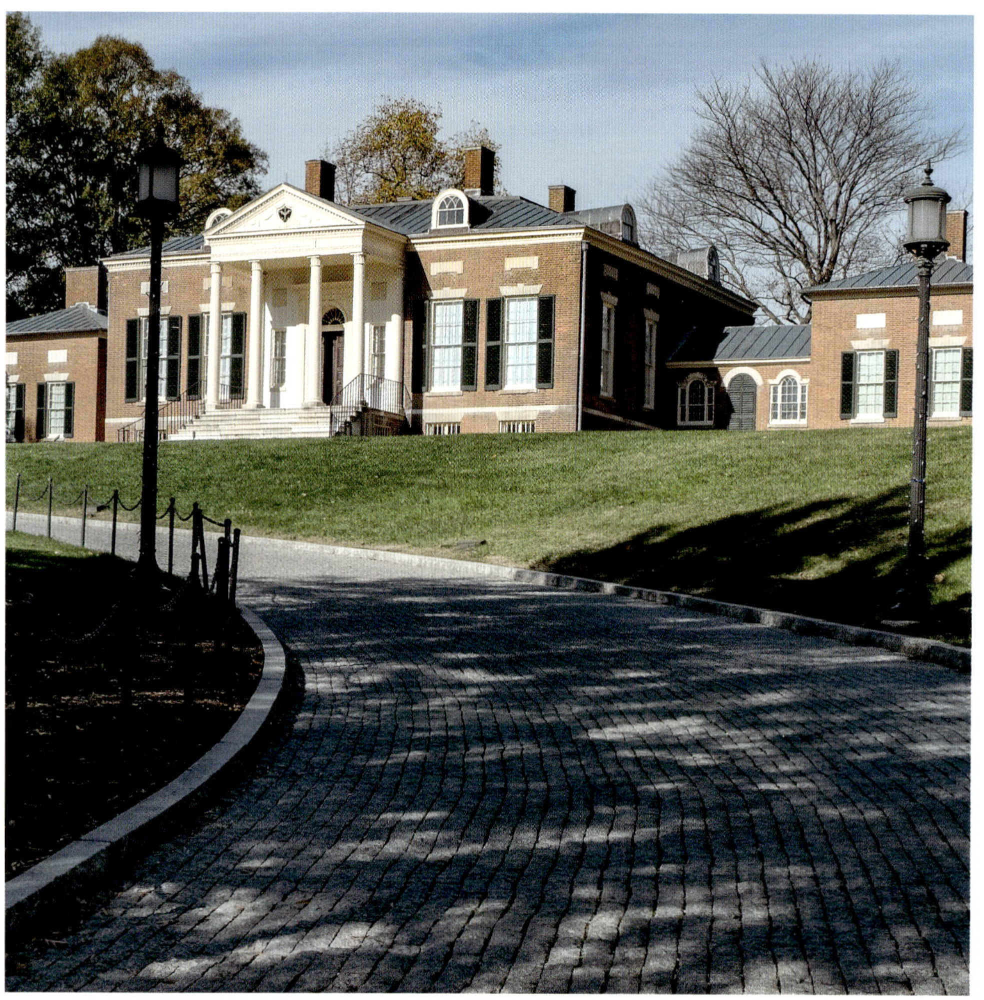

Homewood, Johns Hopkins University

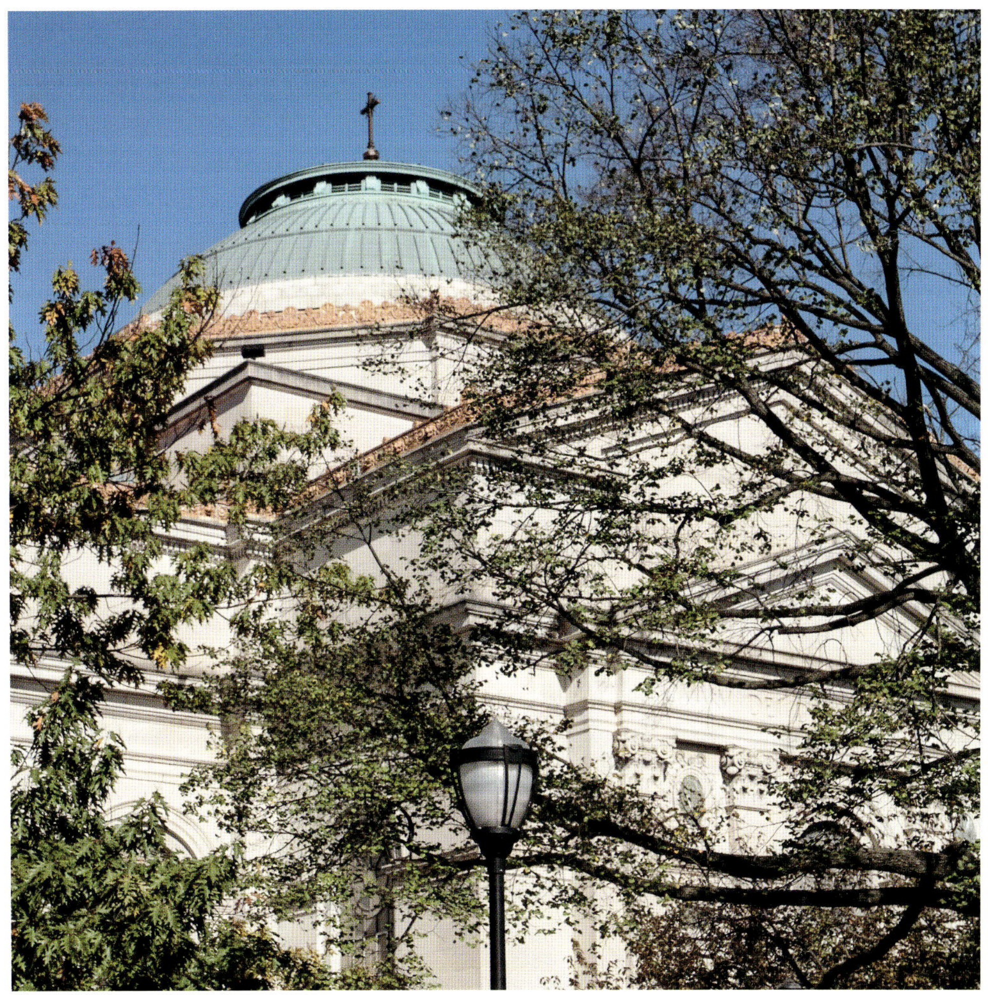

Saints Philip and James Catholic Church

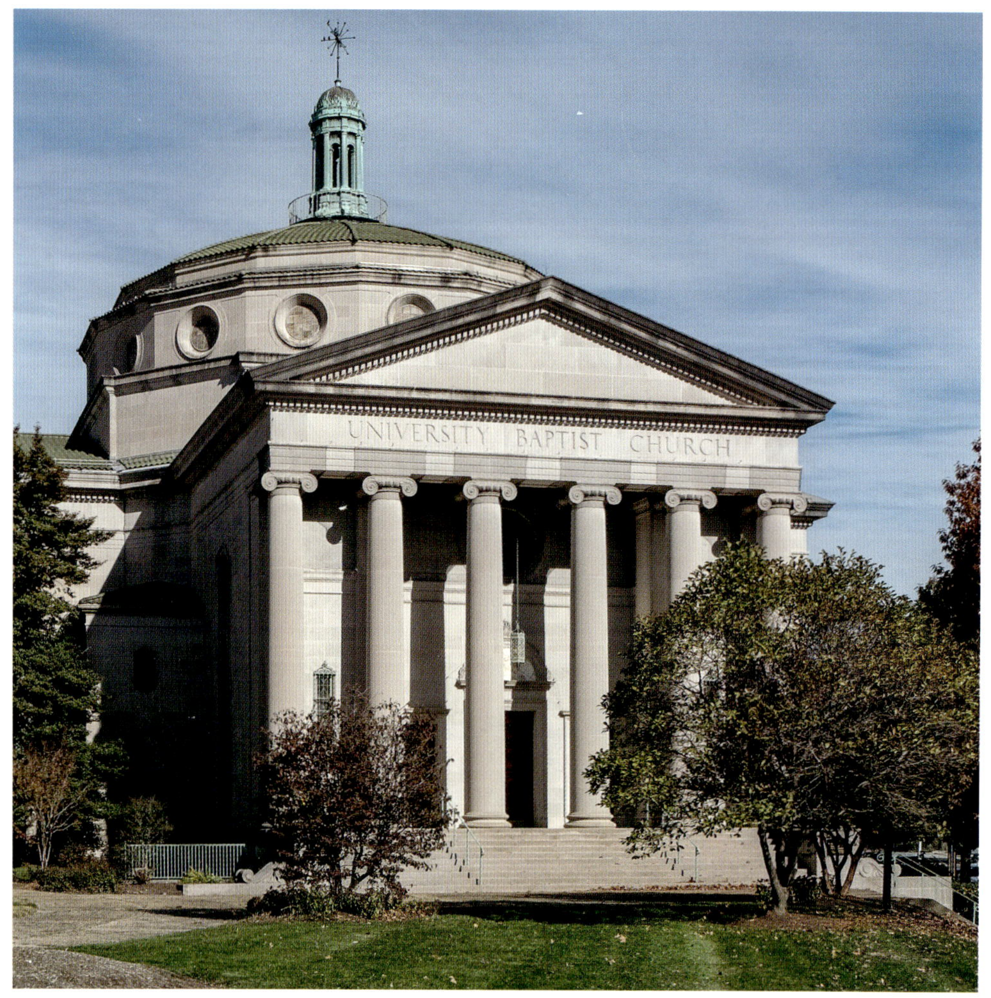

University Baptist Church, Charles Street

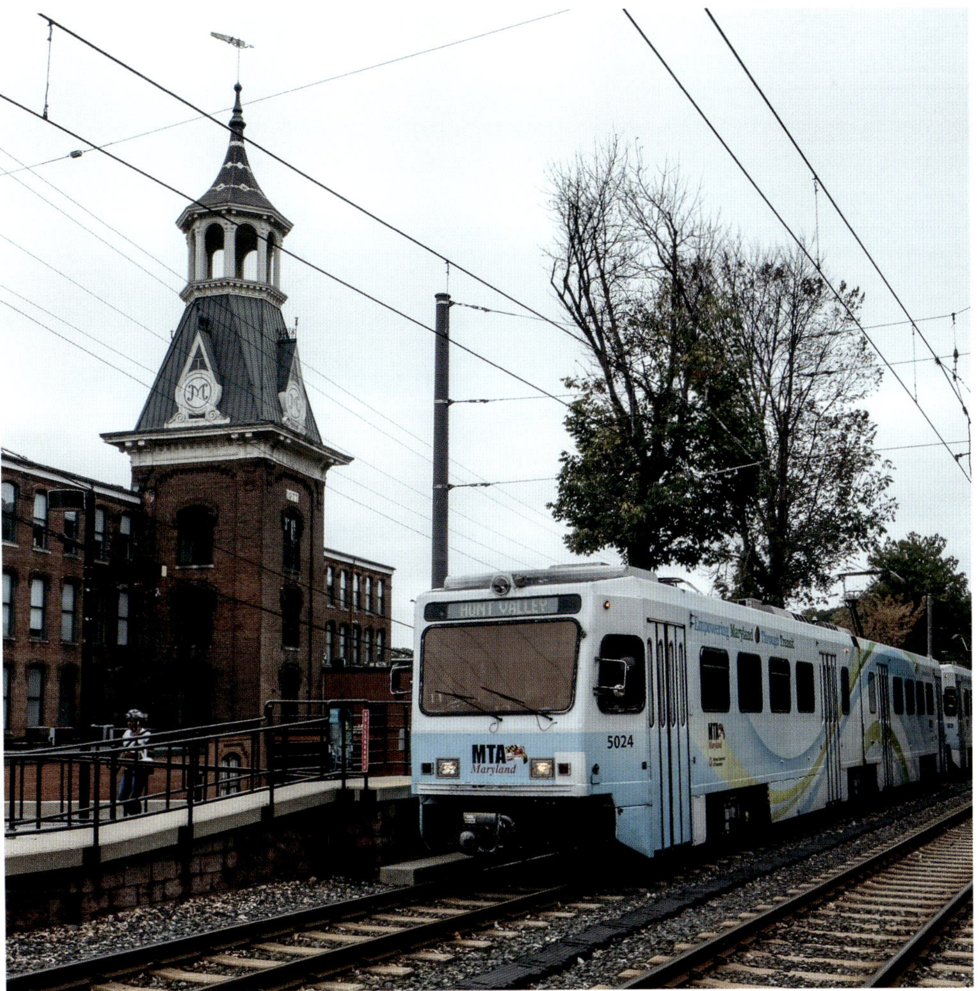

Woodberry

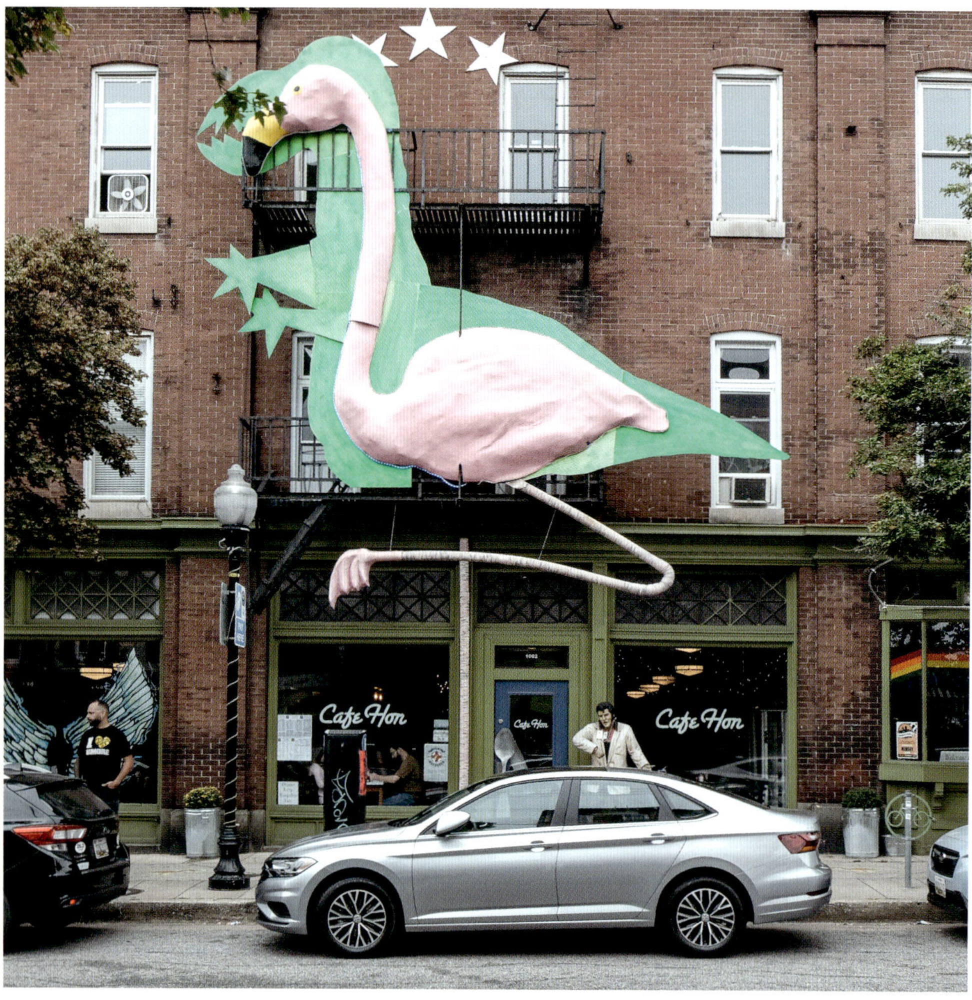

Hampden

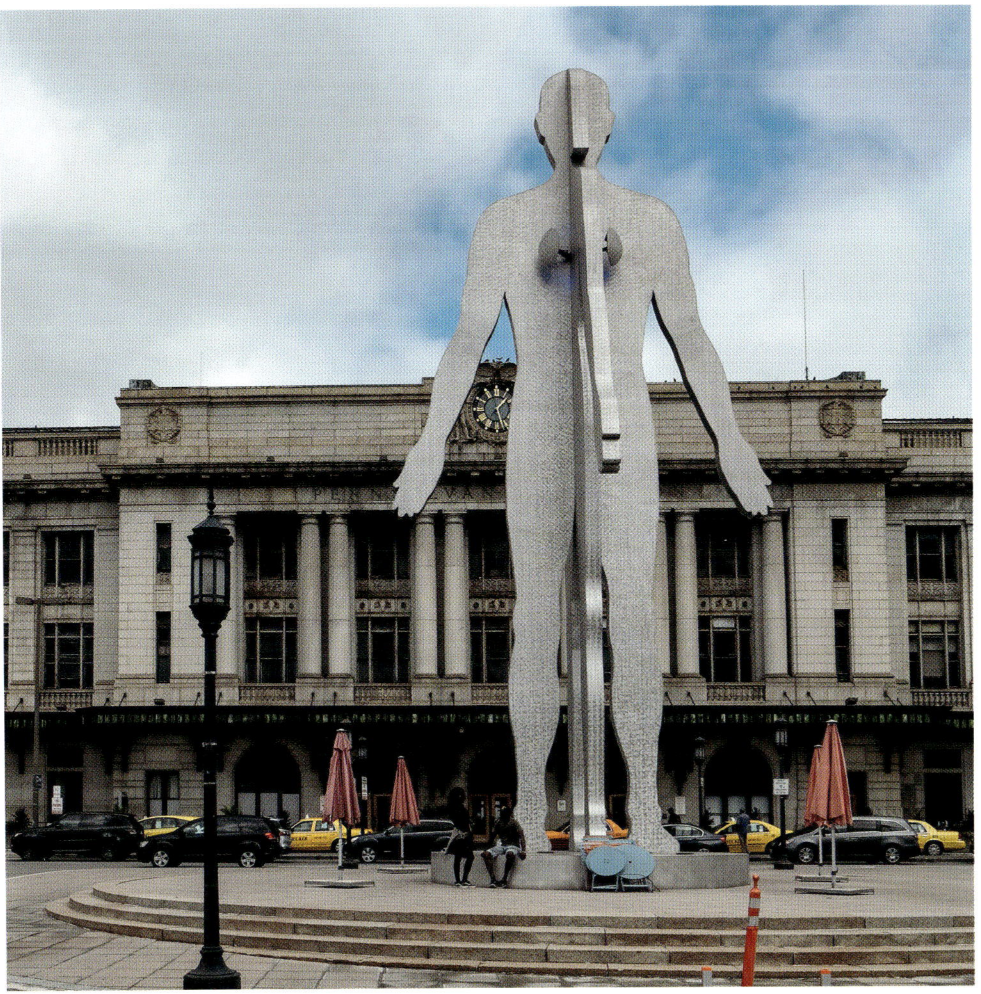

Pennsylvania Station

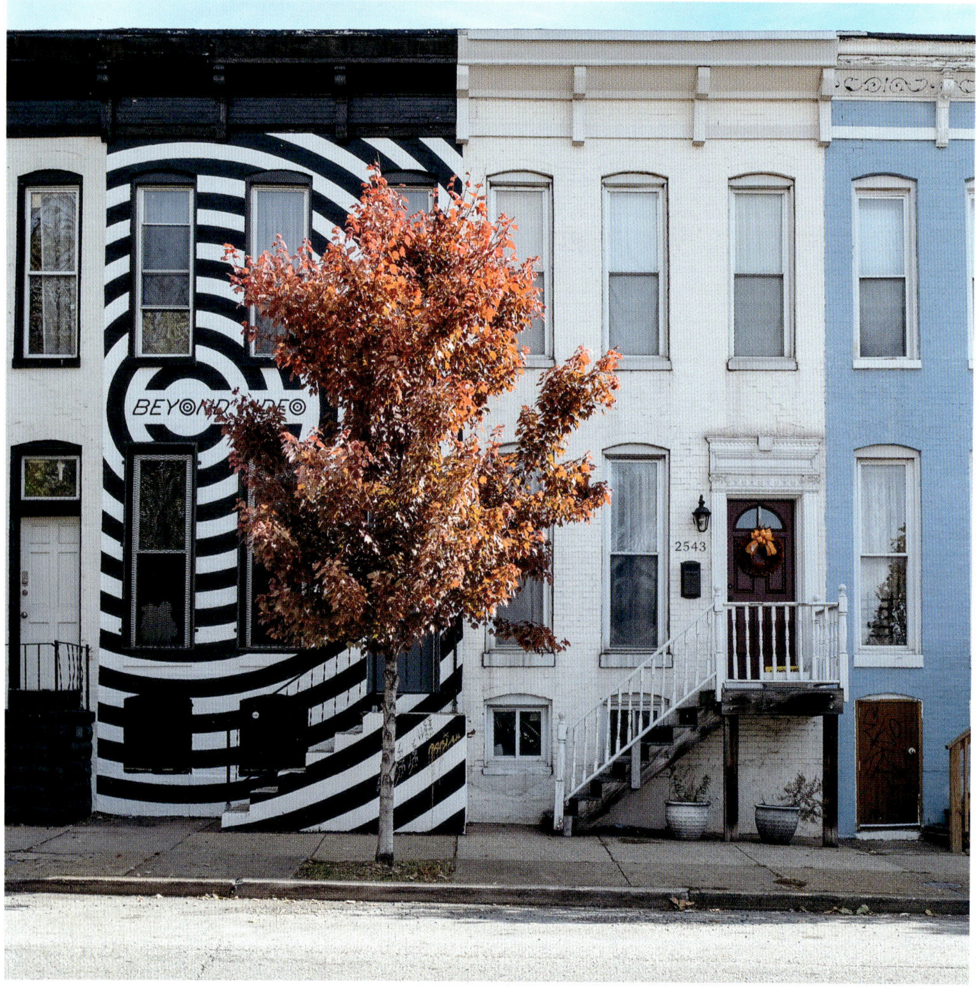

North Howard Street

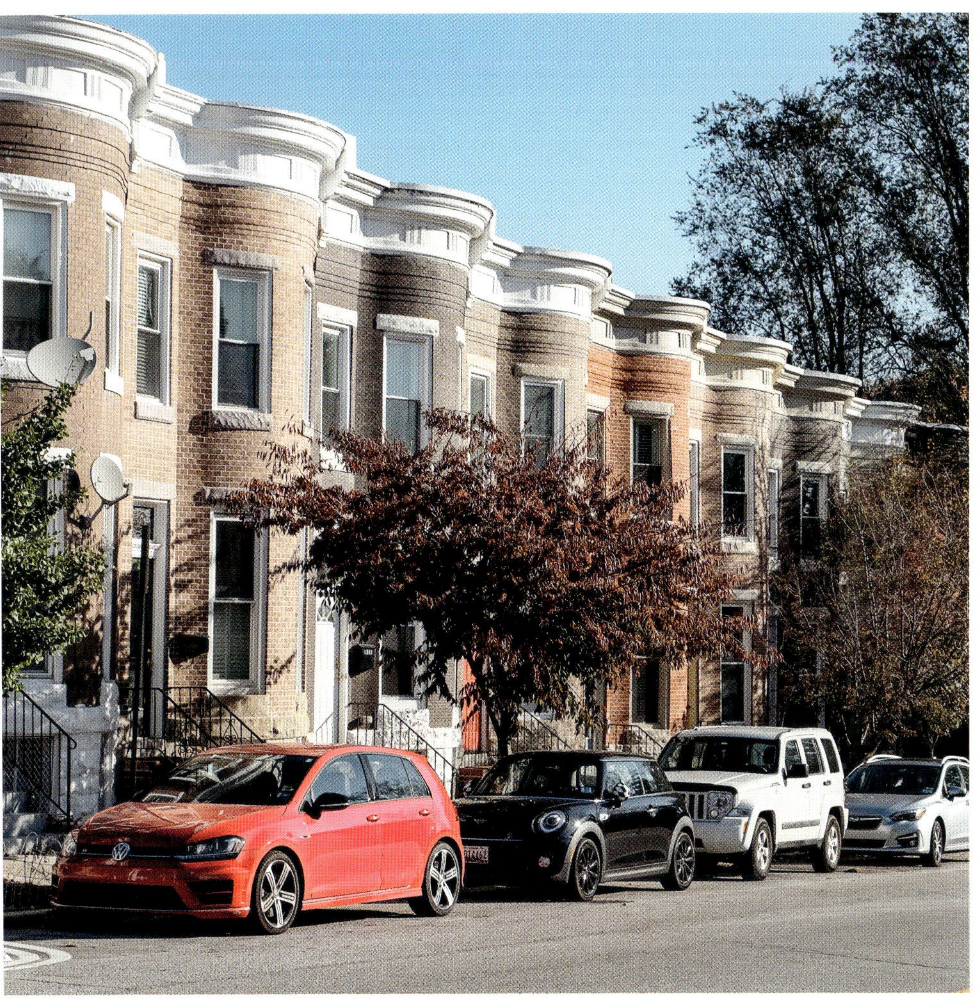

Hampden

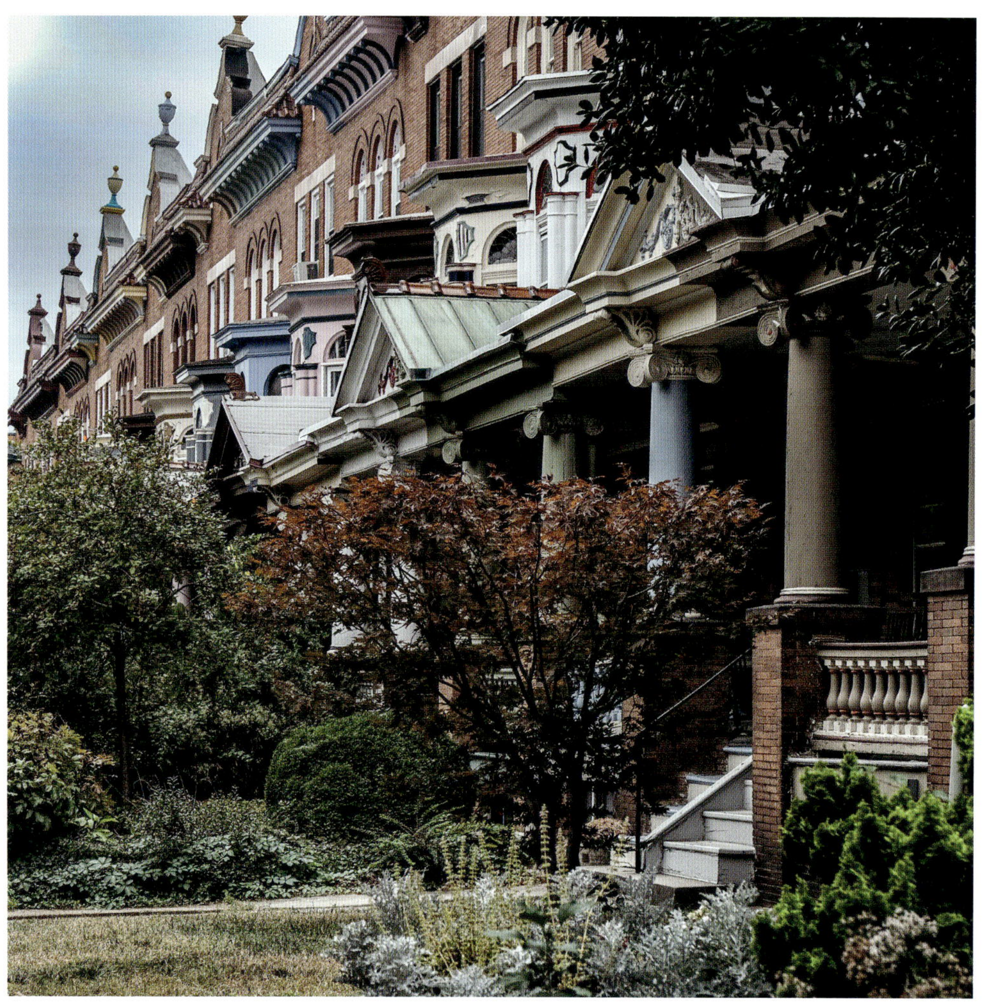

Charles Village

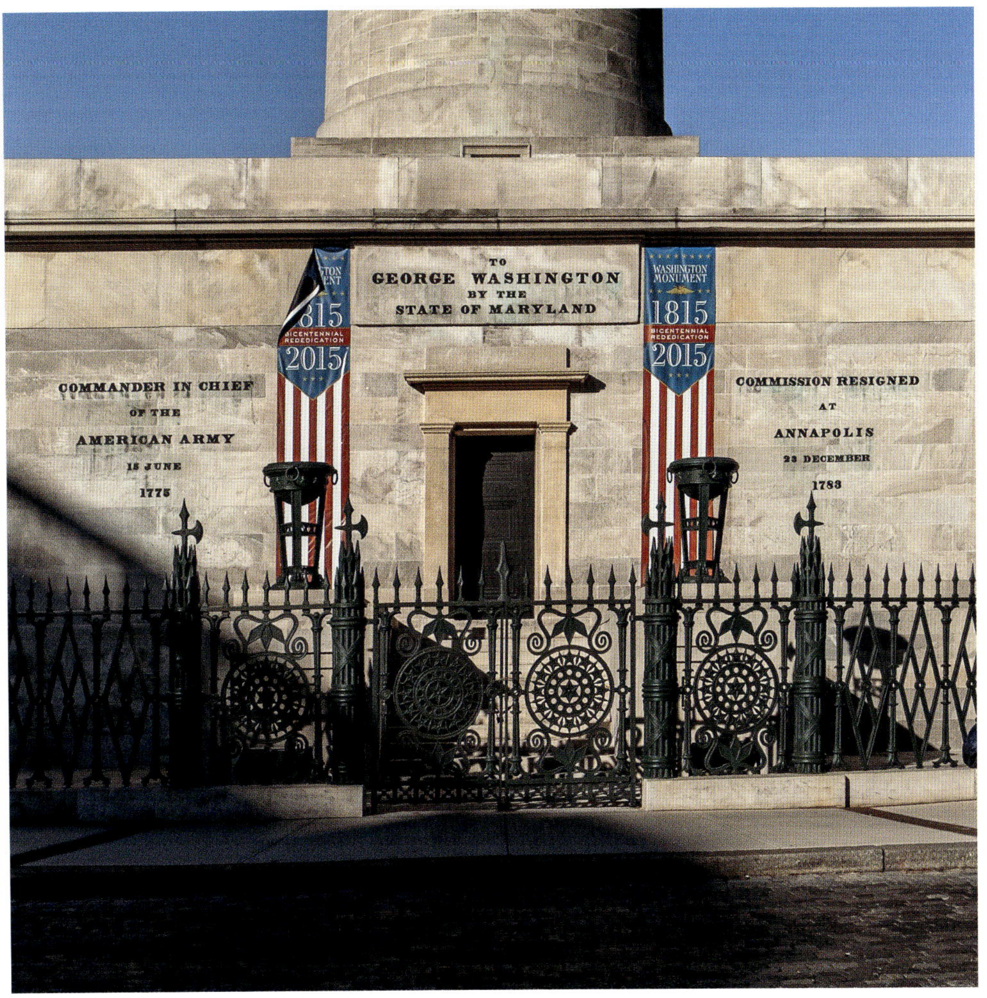

Mount Vernon Square

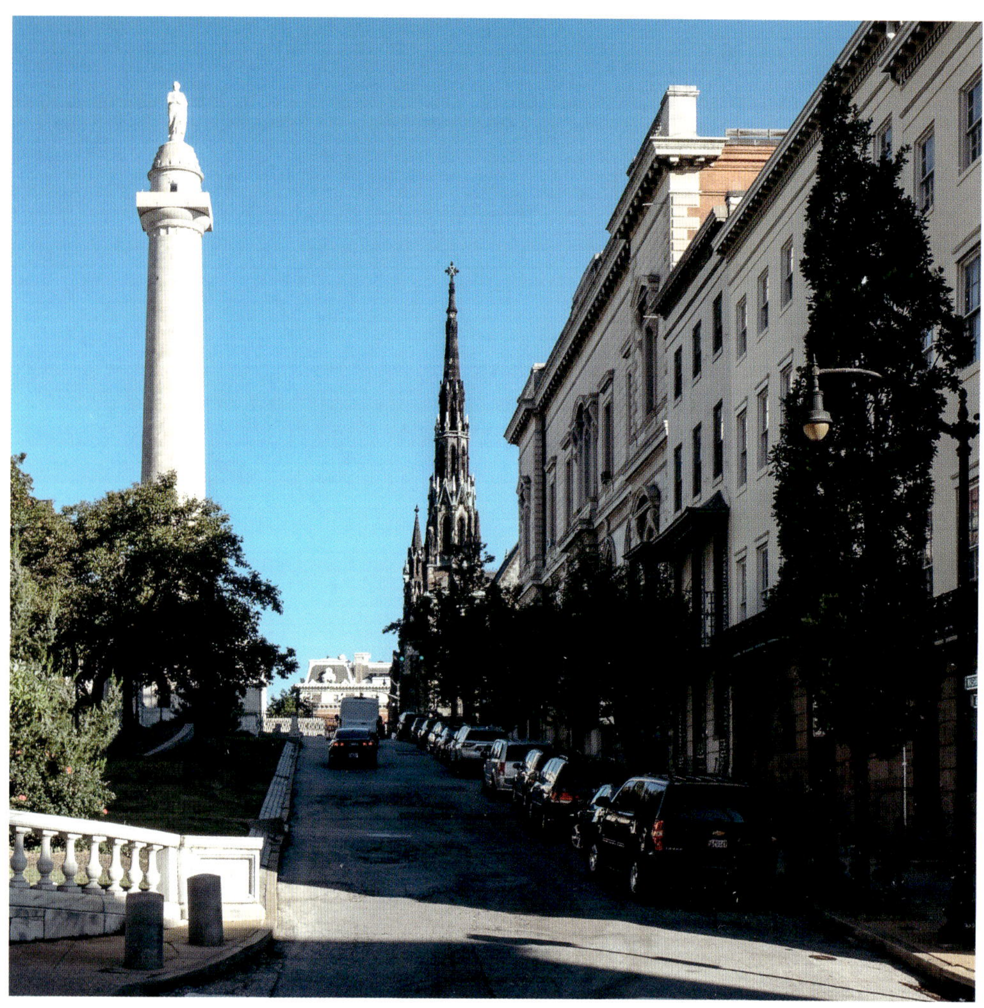

Mount Vernon Square

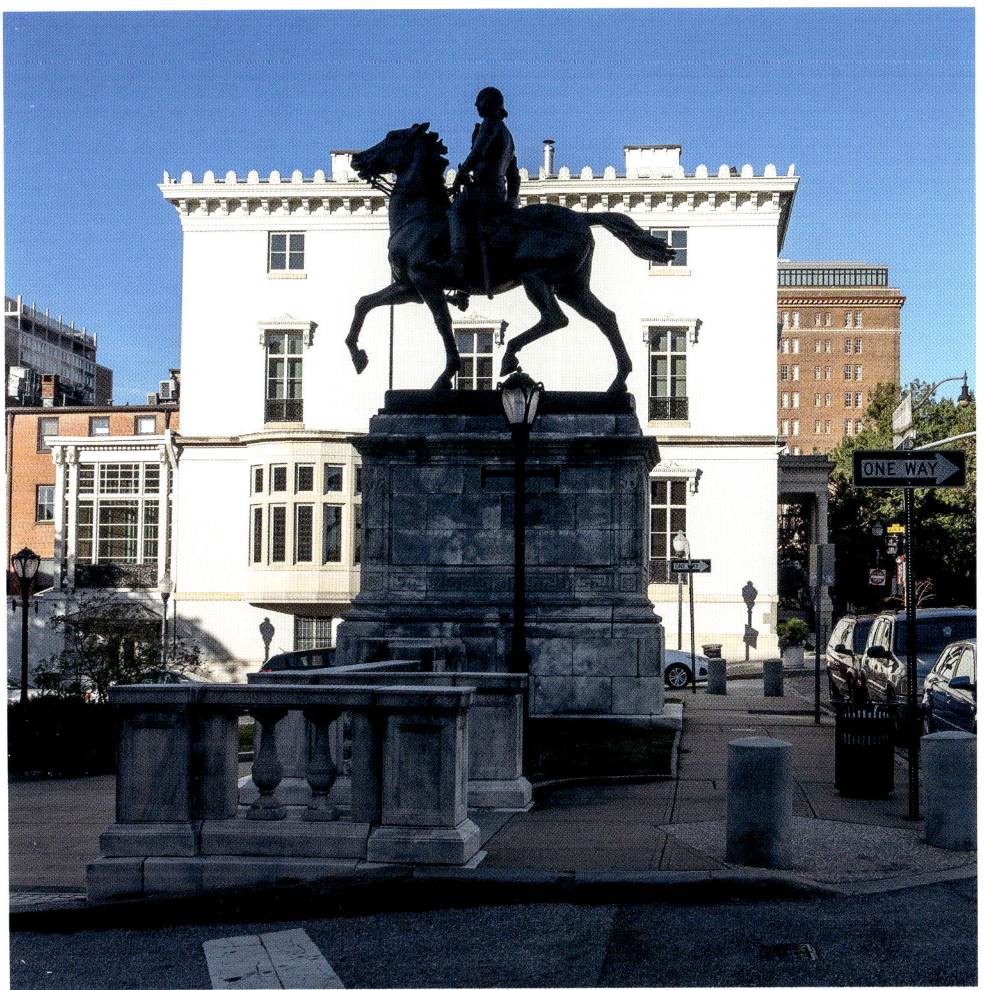

Mount Vernon Square

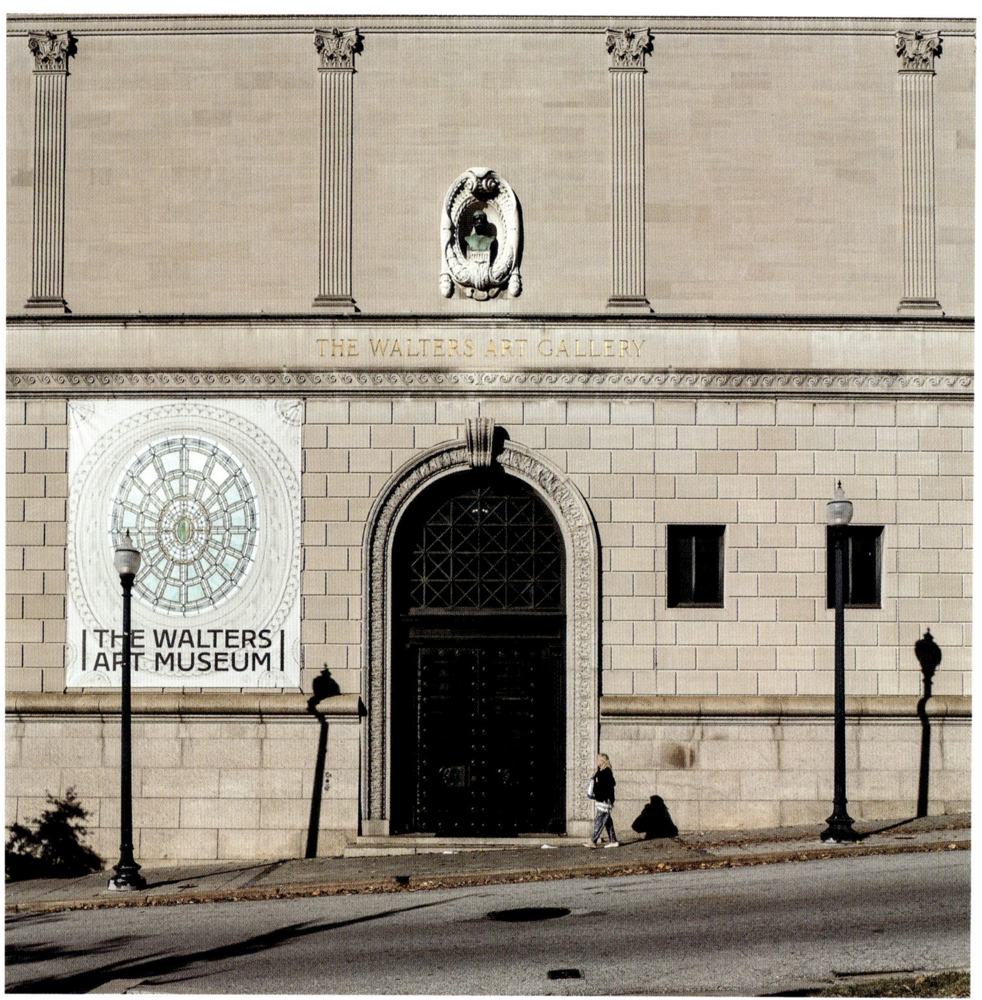

The Walters Art Museum, Mount Vernon Square

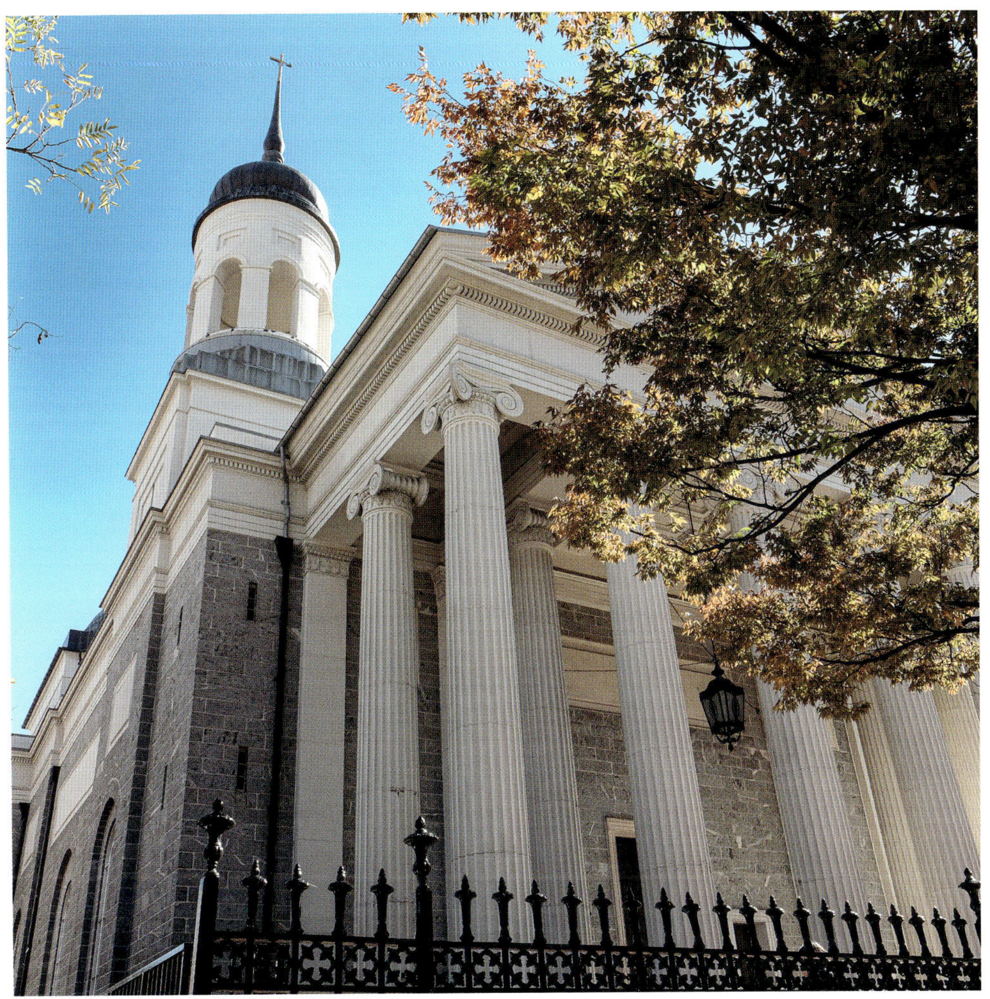

Baltimore Basilica

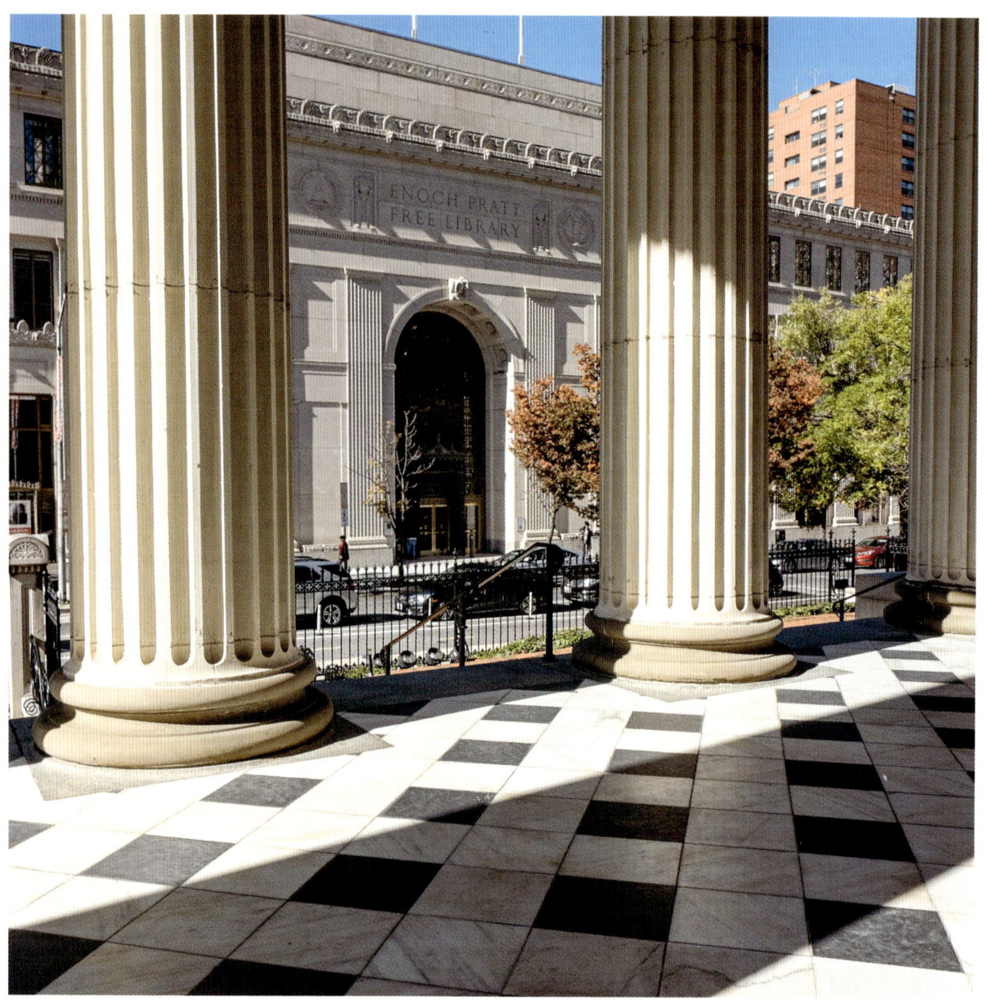

Enoch Pratt Free Library

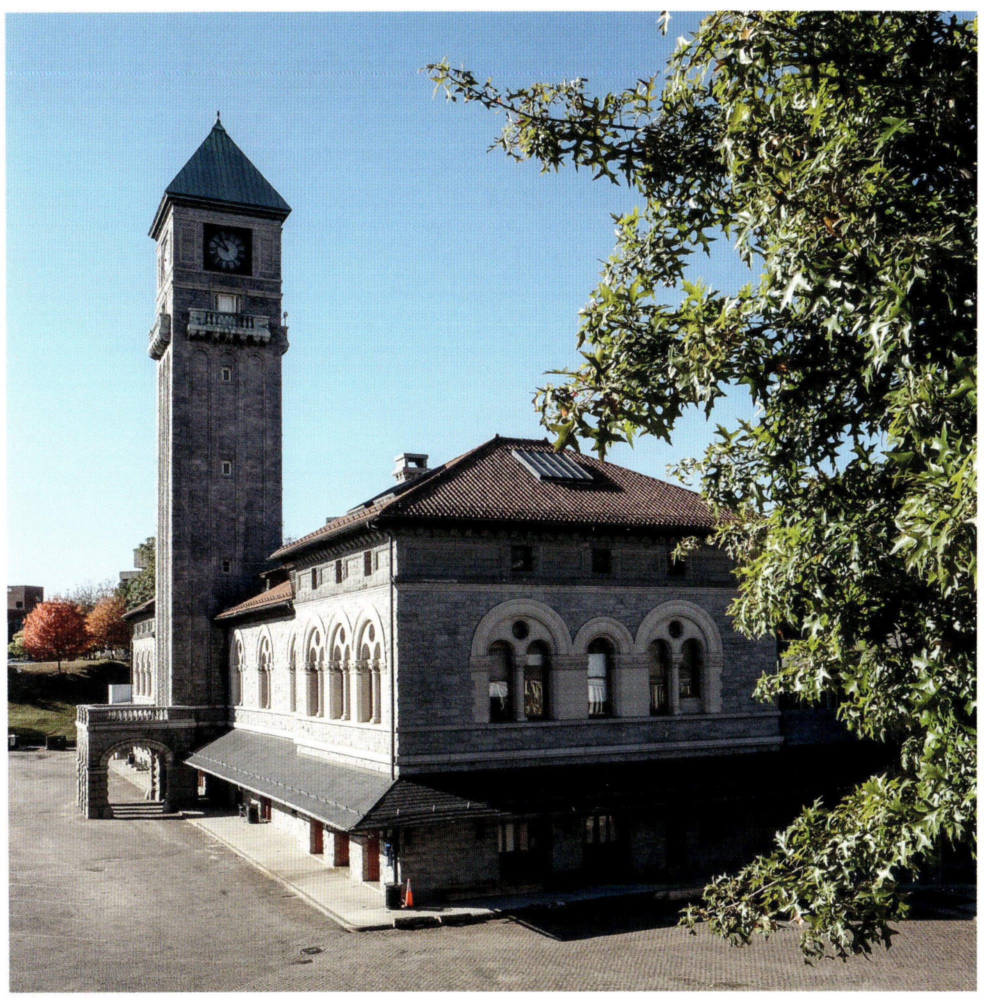

Maryland Institute College of Art, Mount Royal Station

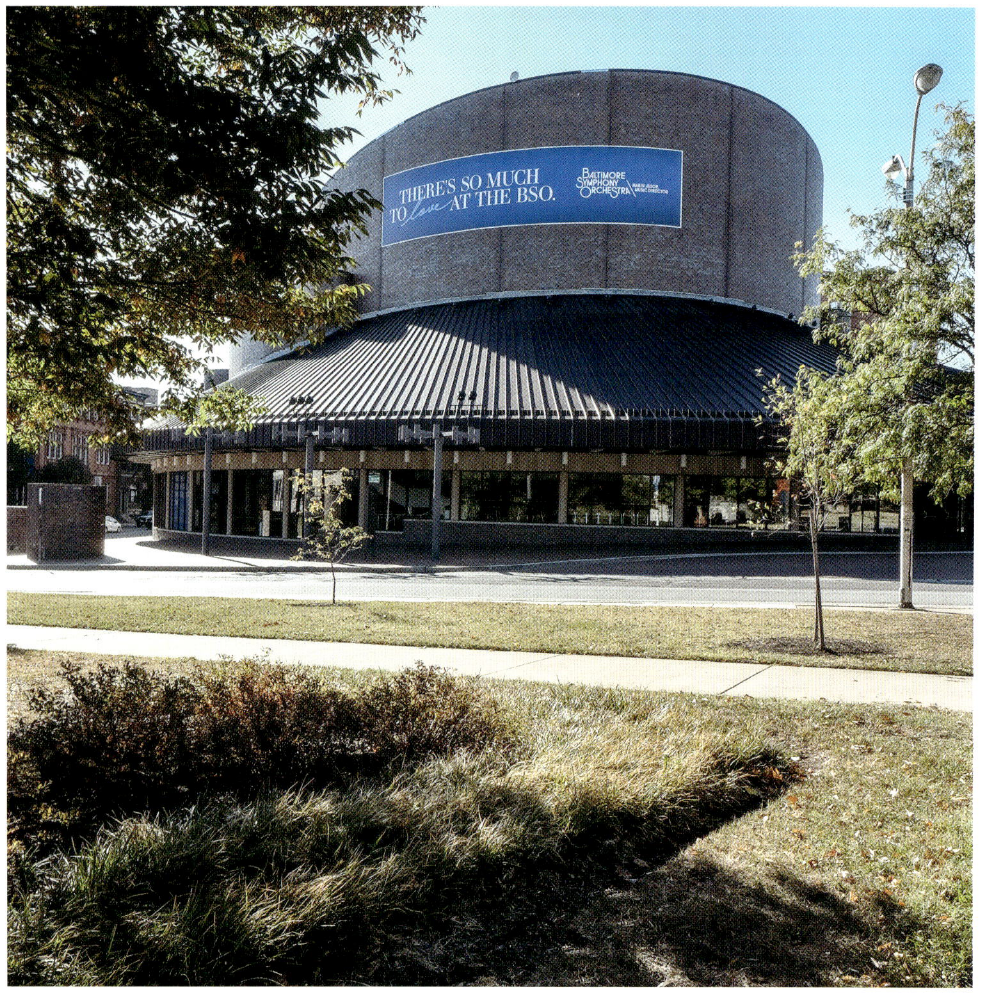

Joseph Meyerhoff Symphony Hall

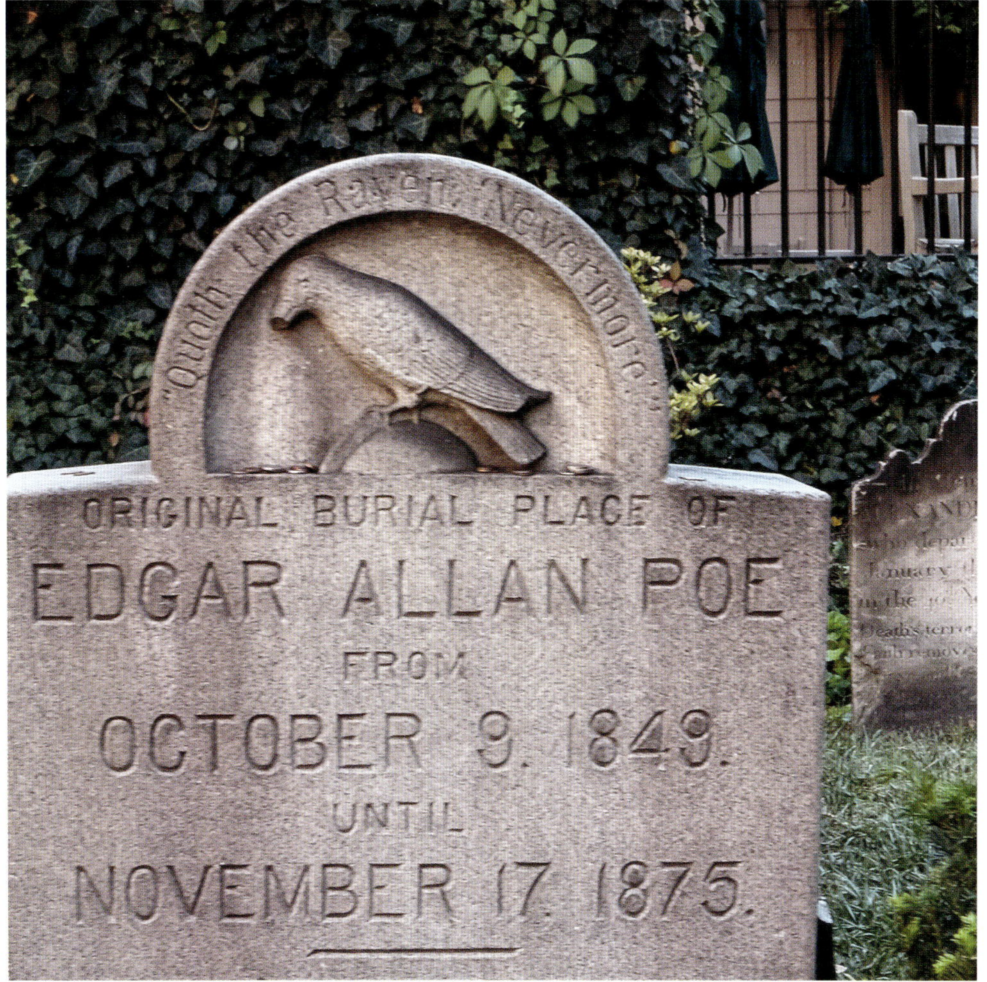

Edgar Allan Poe's gravesite, Westminster Cemetery

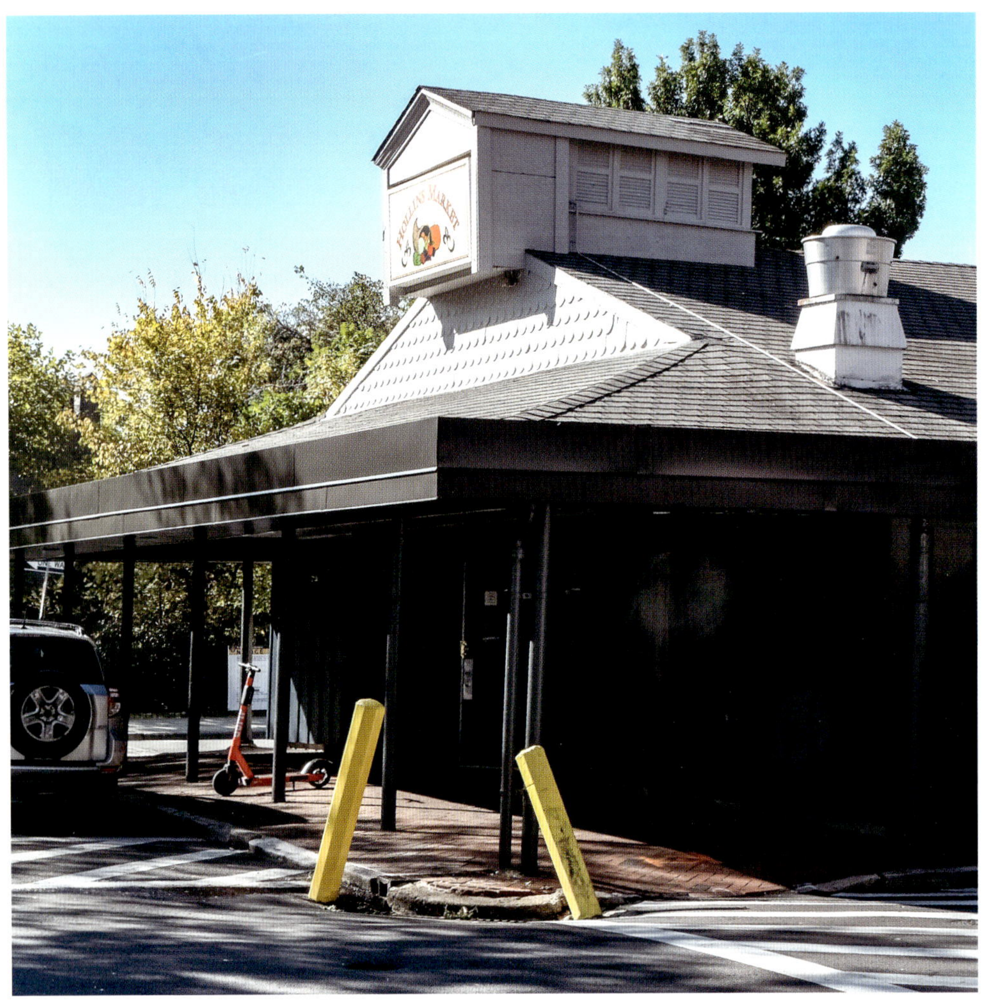

Hollins Market

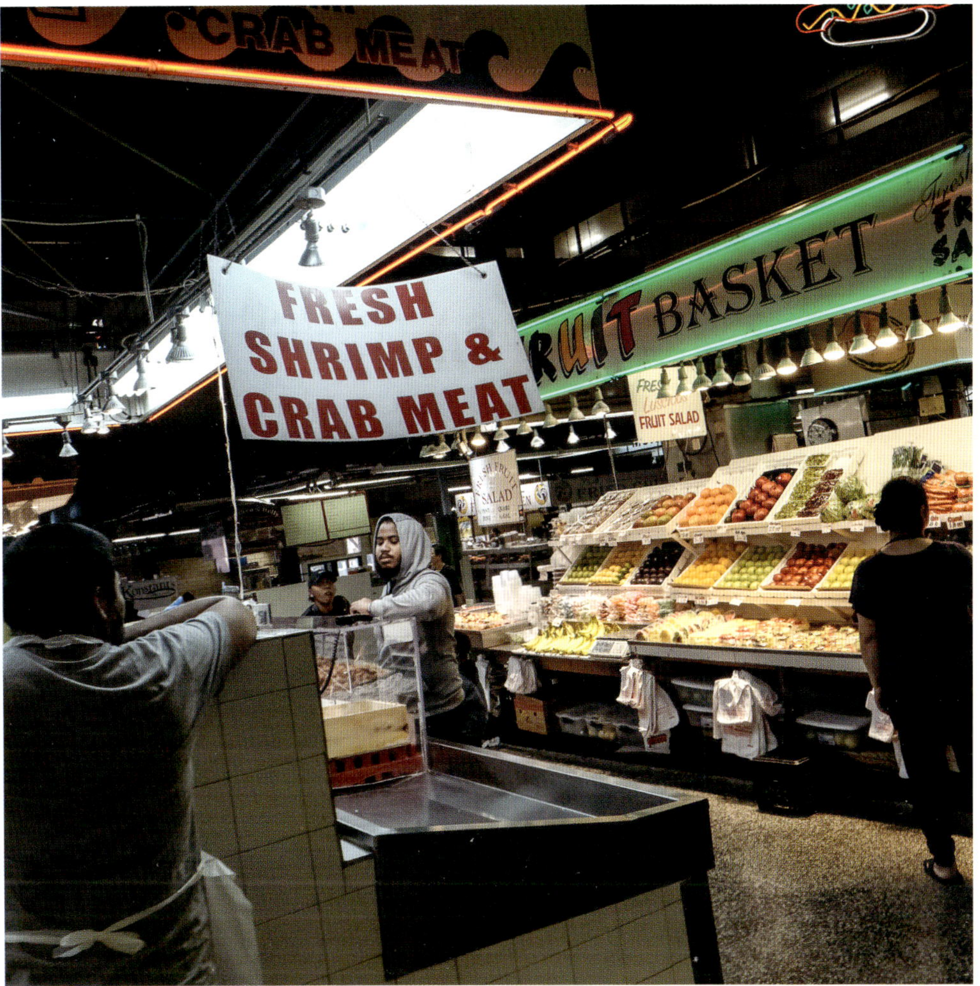

Lexington Market

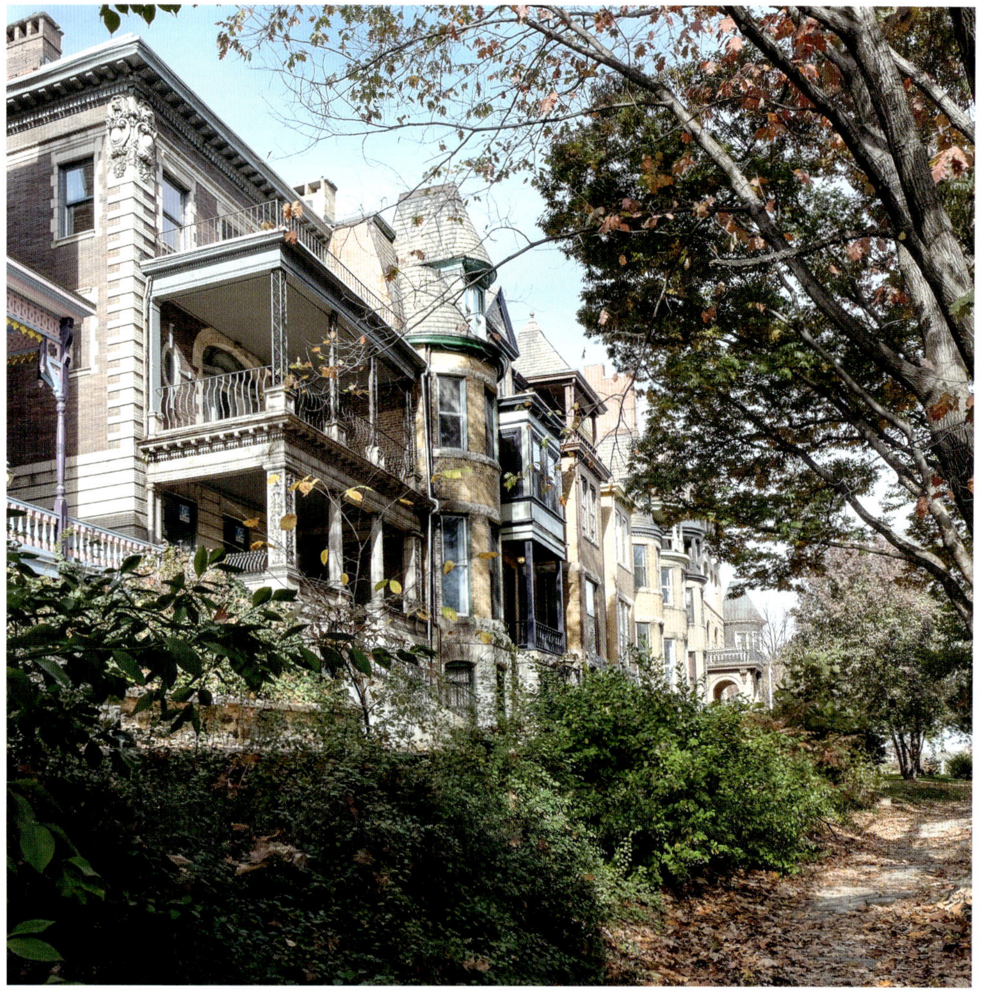

Mount Royal Terrace

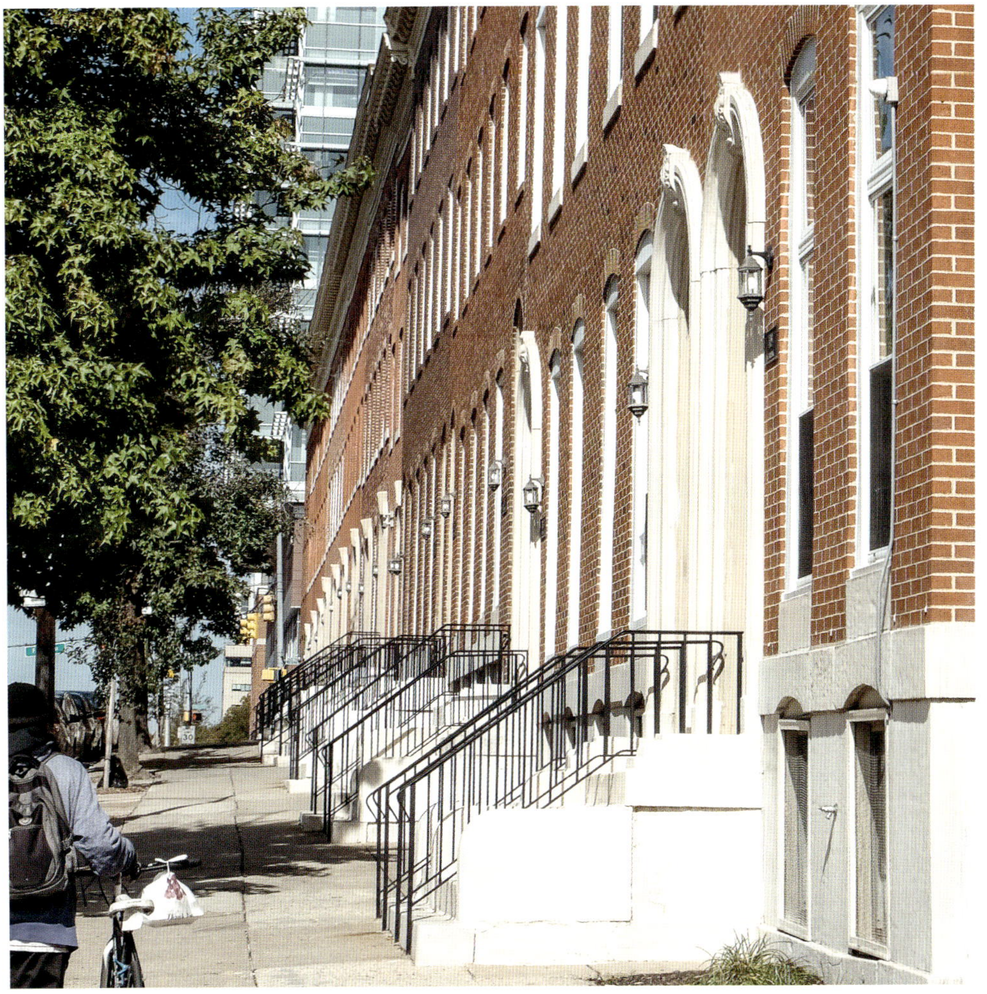

North Broadway, Butcher's Hill

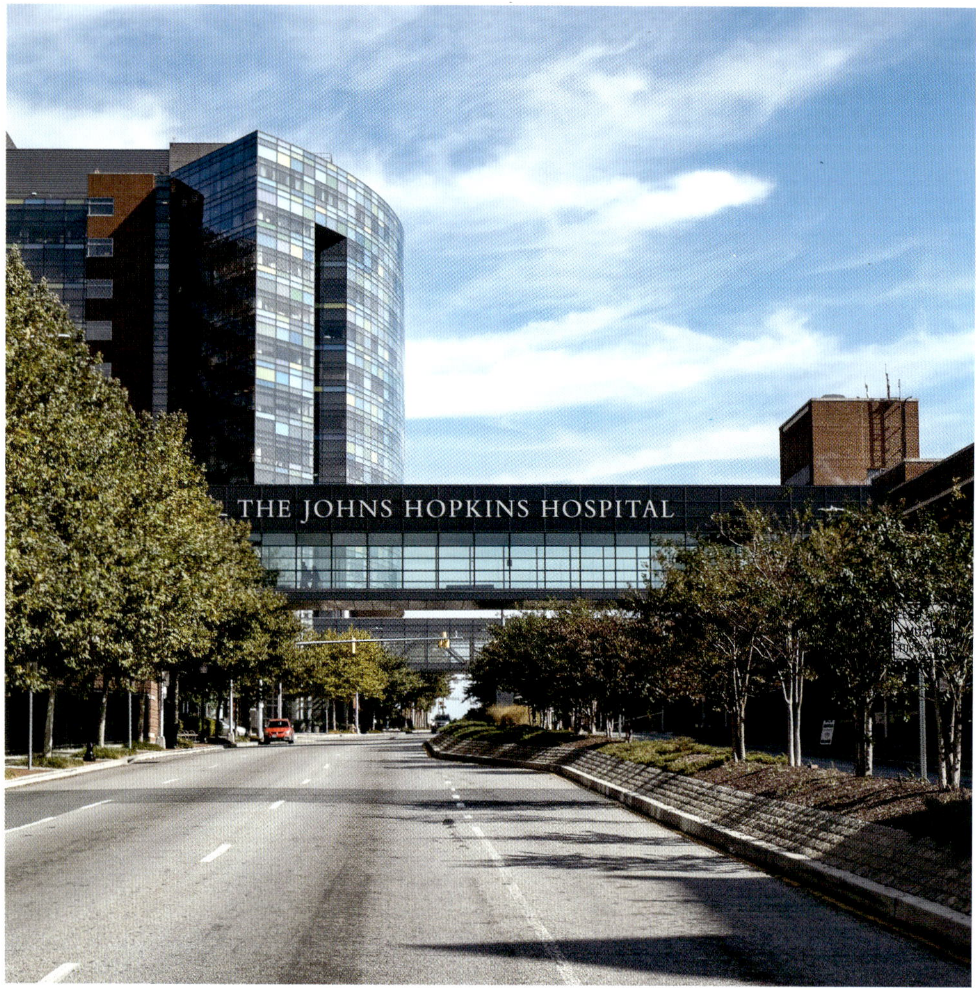

Johns Hopkins Medical Center

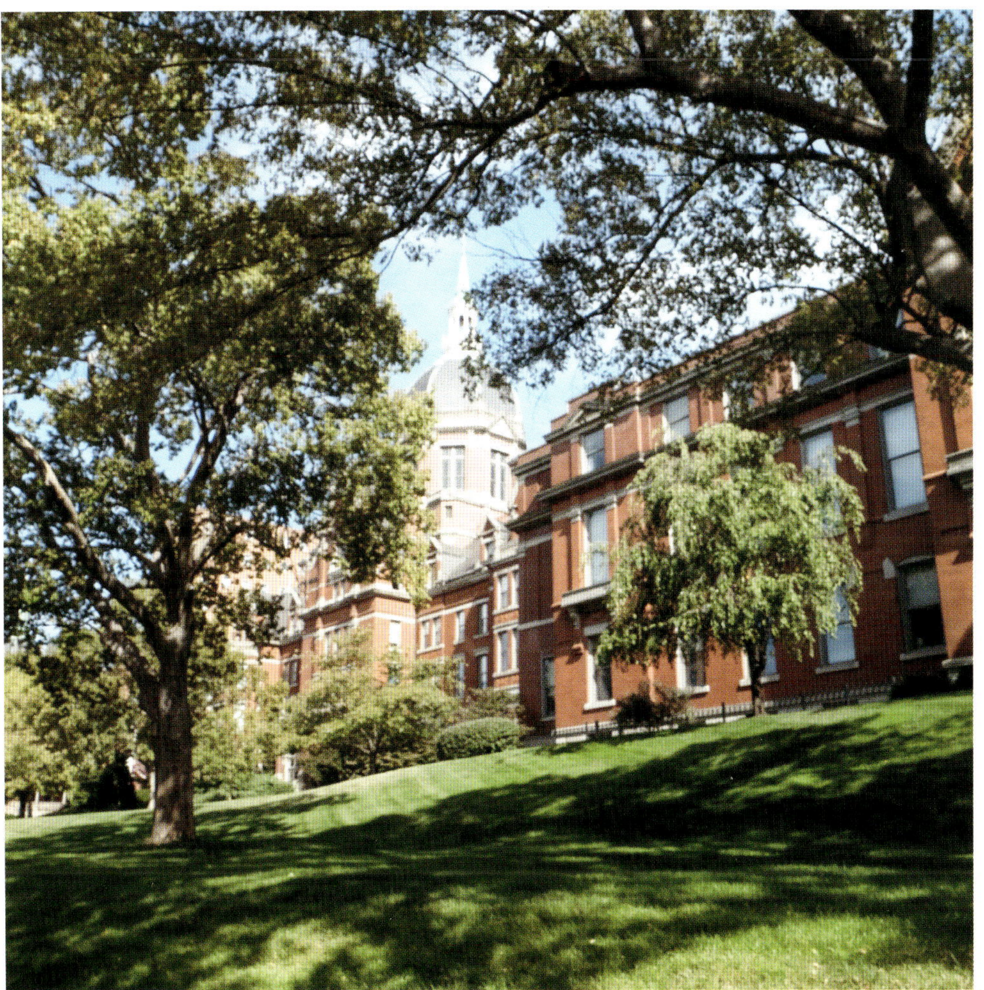

Johns Hopkins Medical Center

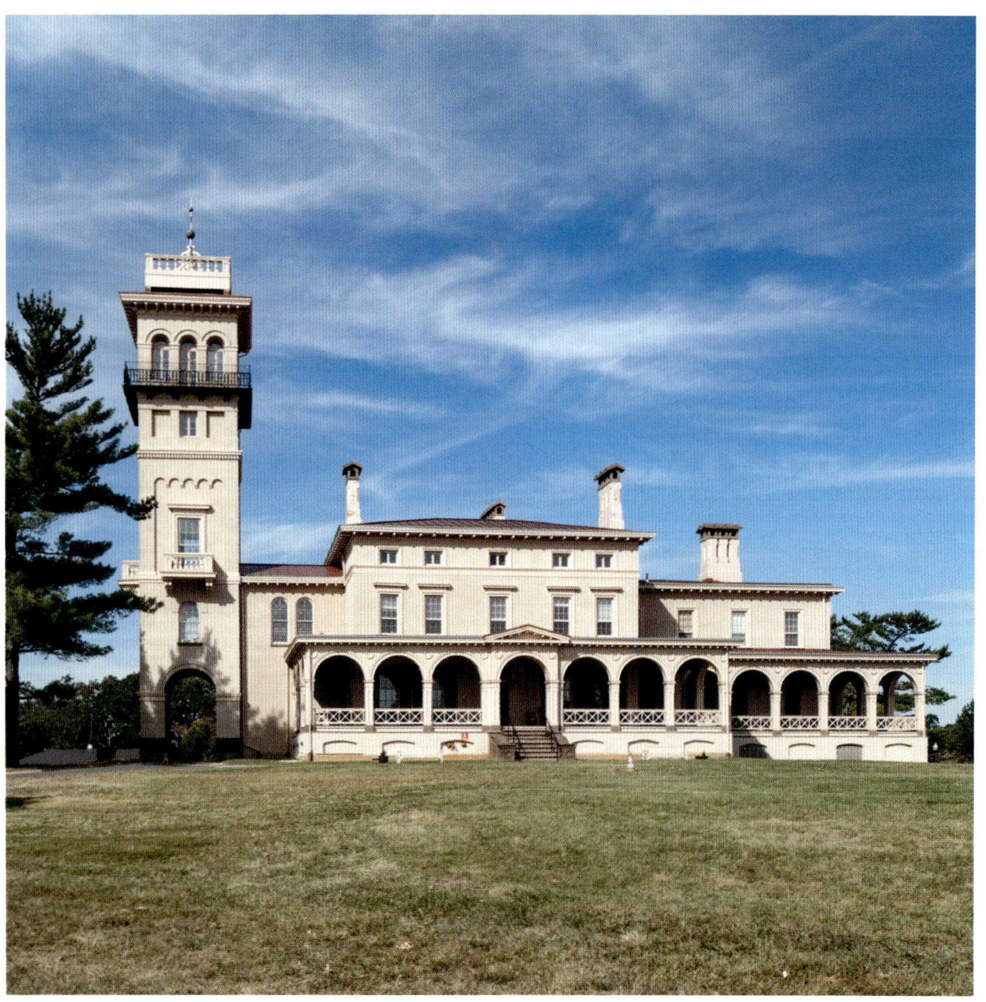

Clifton Mansion, Clifton Park

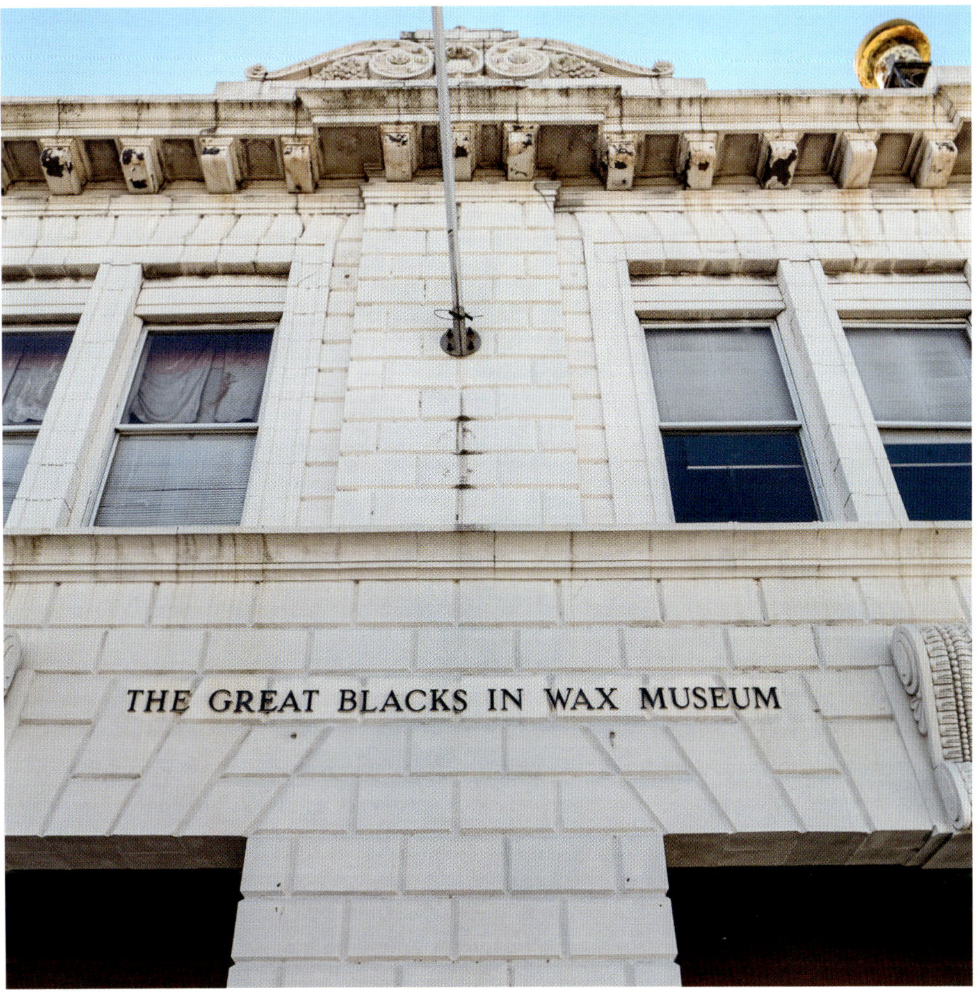

National Great Blacks in Wax Museum, East North Street

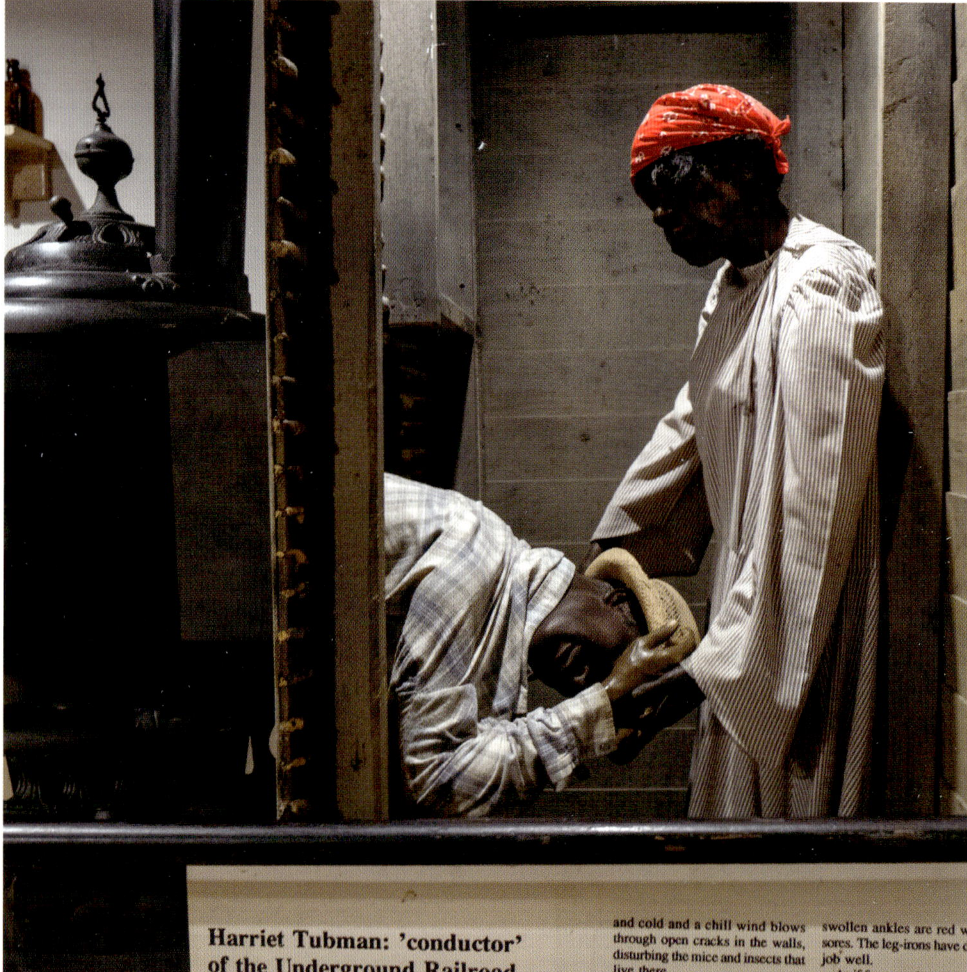

National Great Blacks in Wax Museum, East North Street

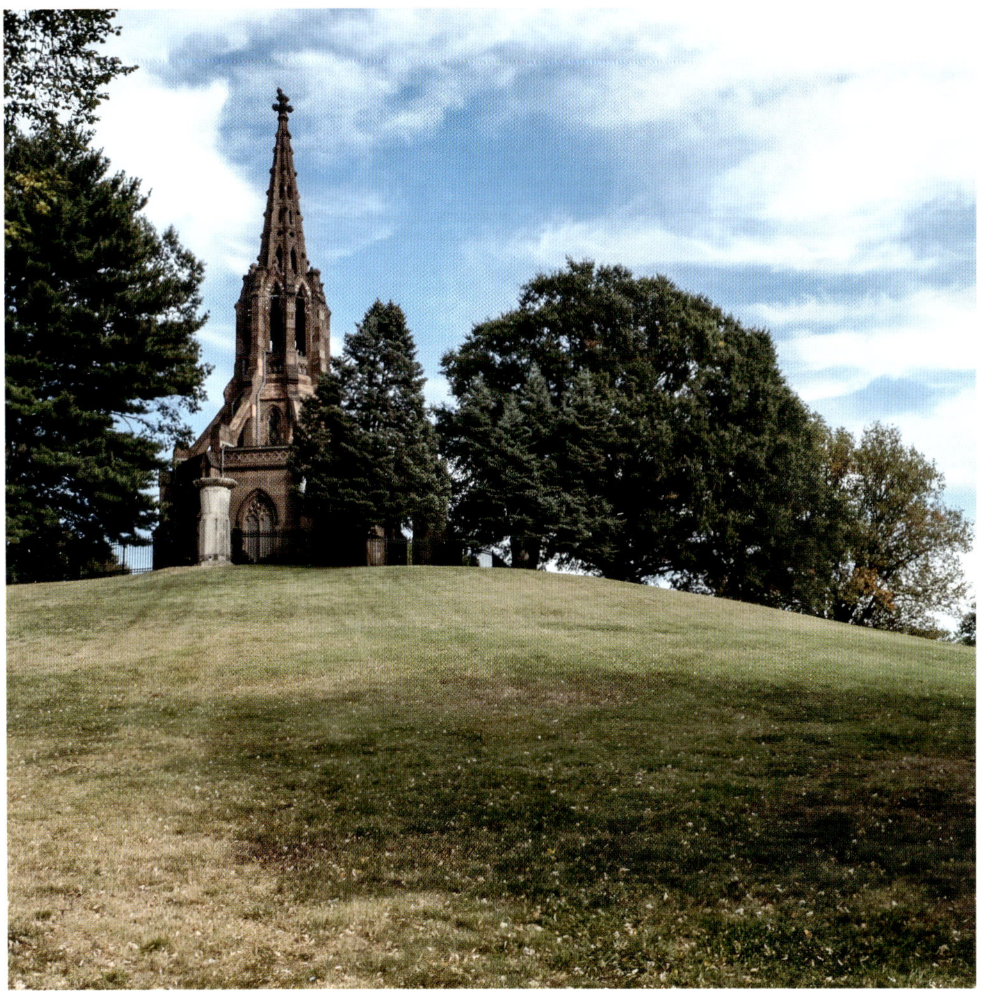

Greenmount Cemetery

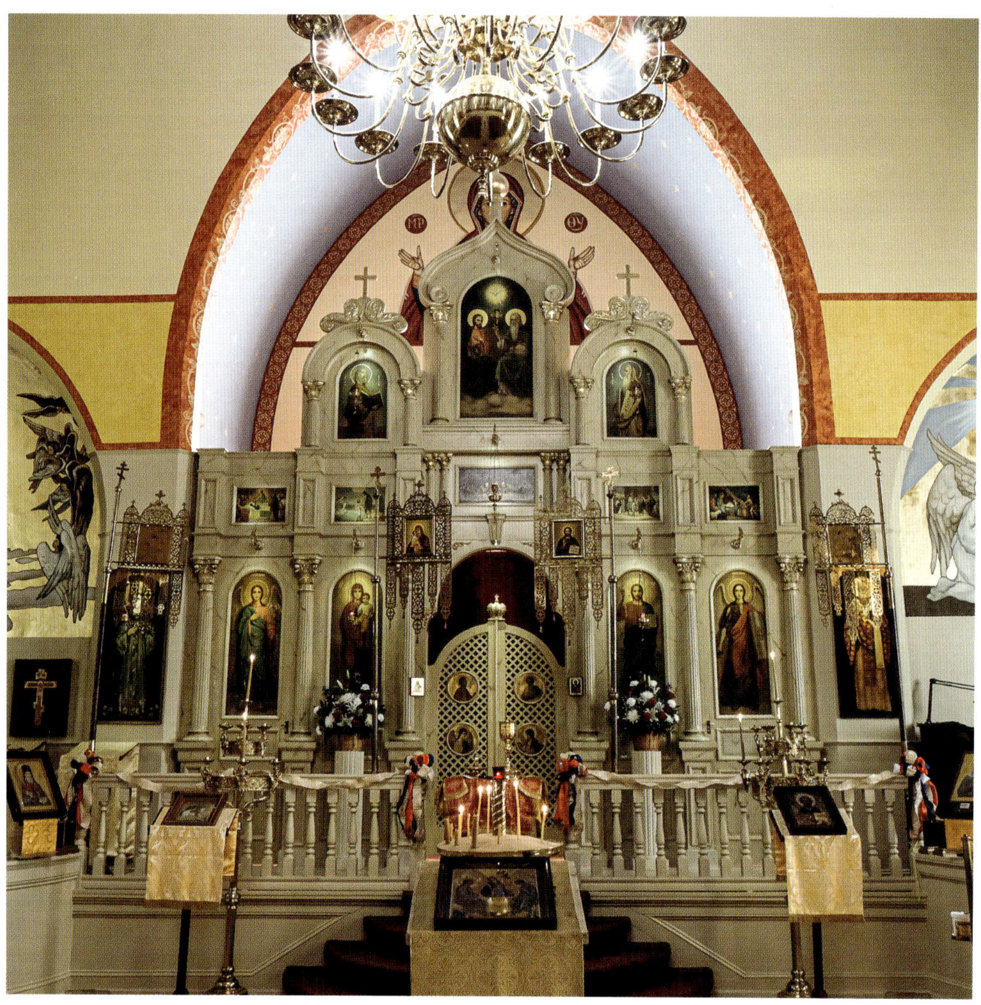

Transfiguration of Our Lord Russian Orthodox Church

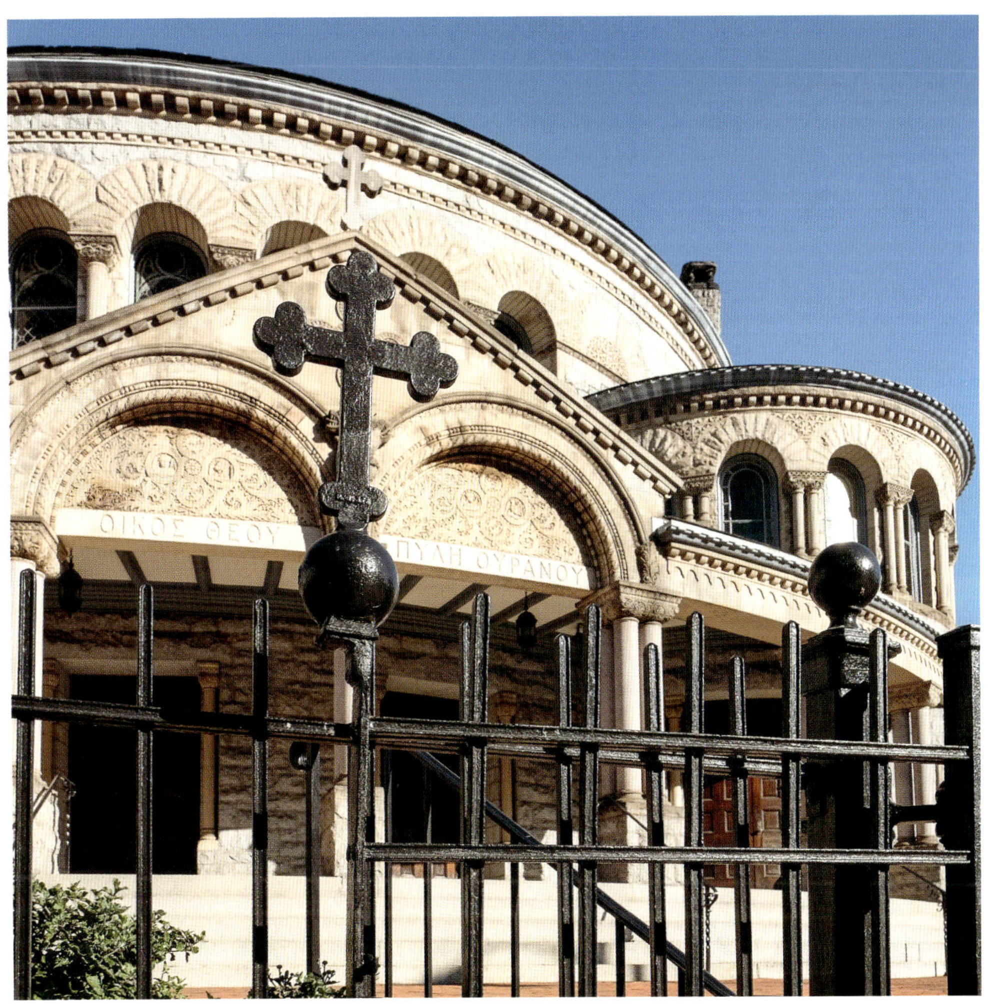

Greek Orthodox Cathedral of the Annunciation

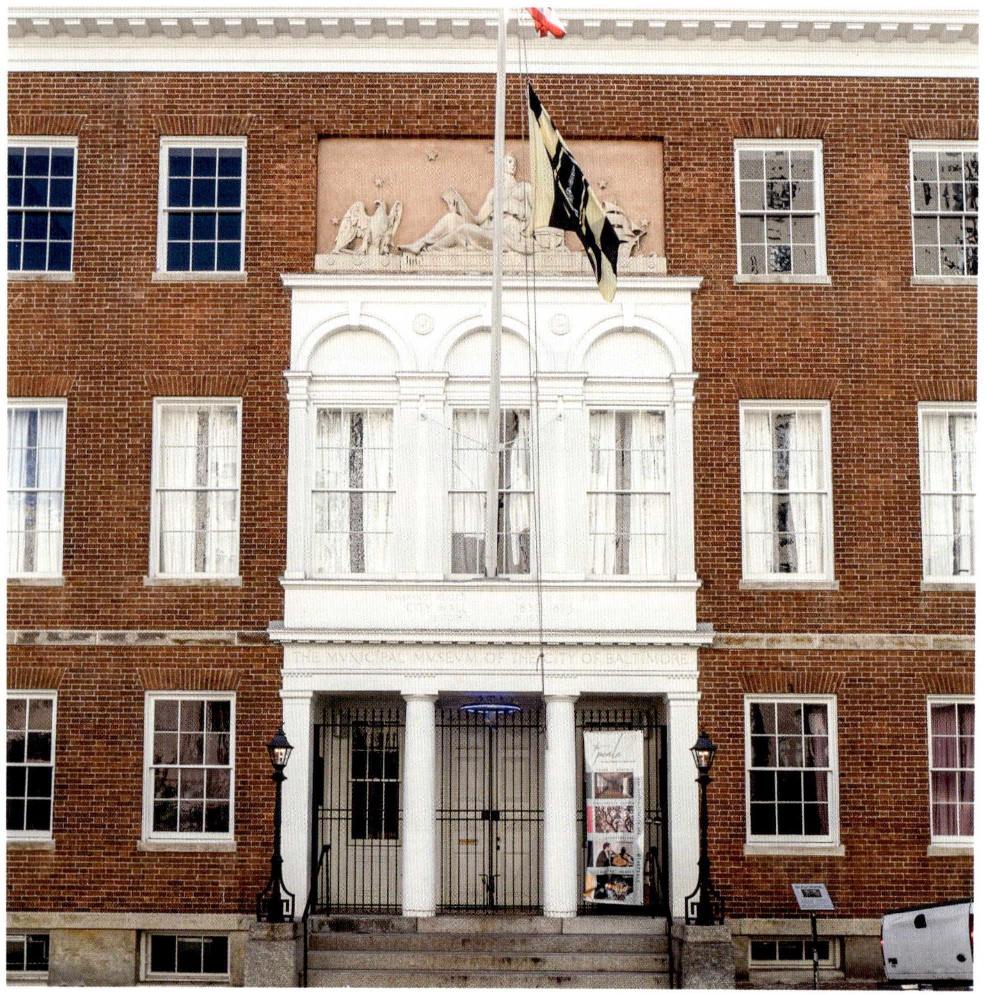

Peale Center for Baltimore History and Architecture

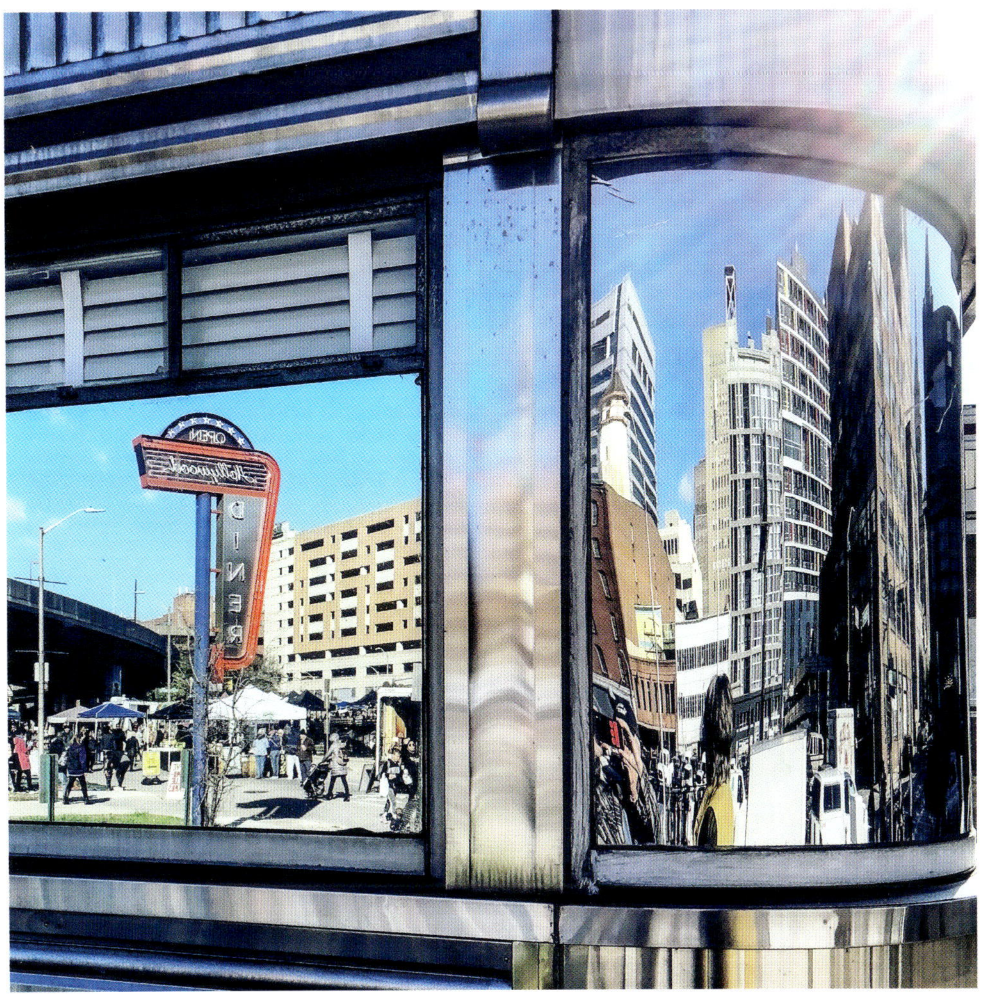

Holiday Diner, Saratoga Street

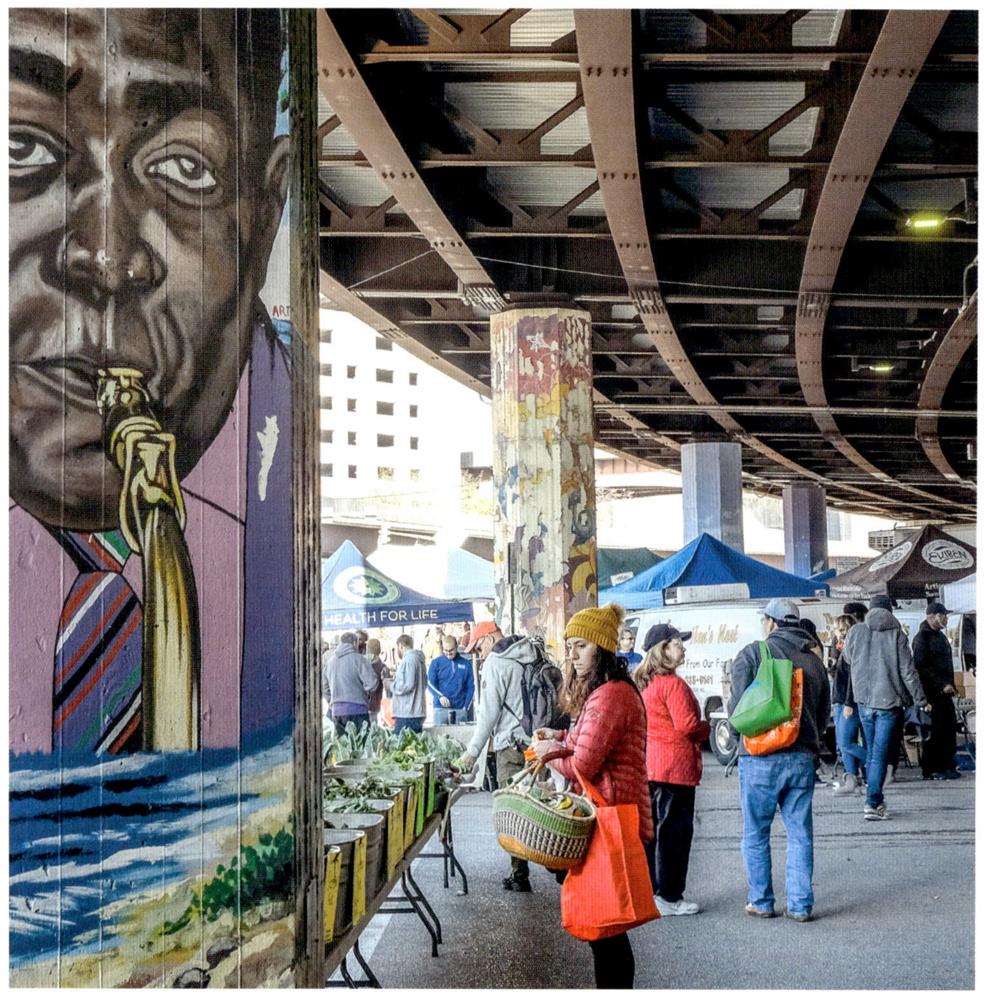

Baltimore Farmers' Market, Saratoga Street

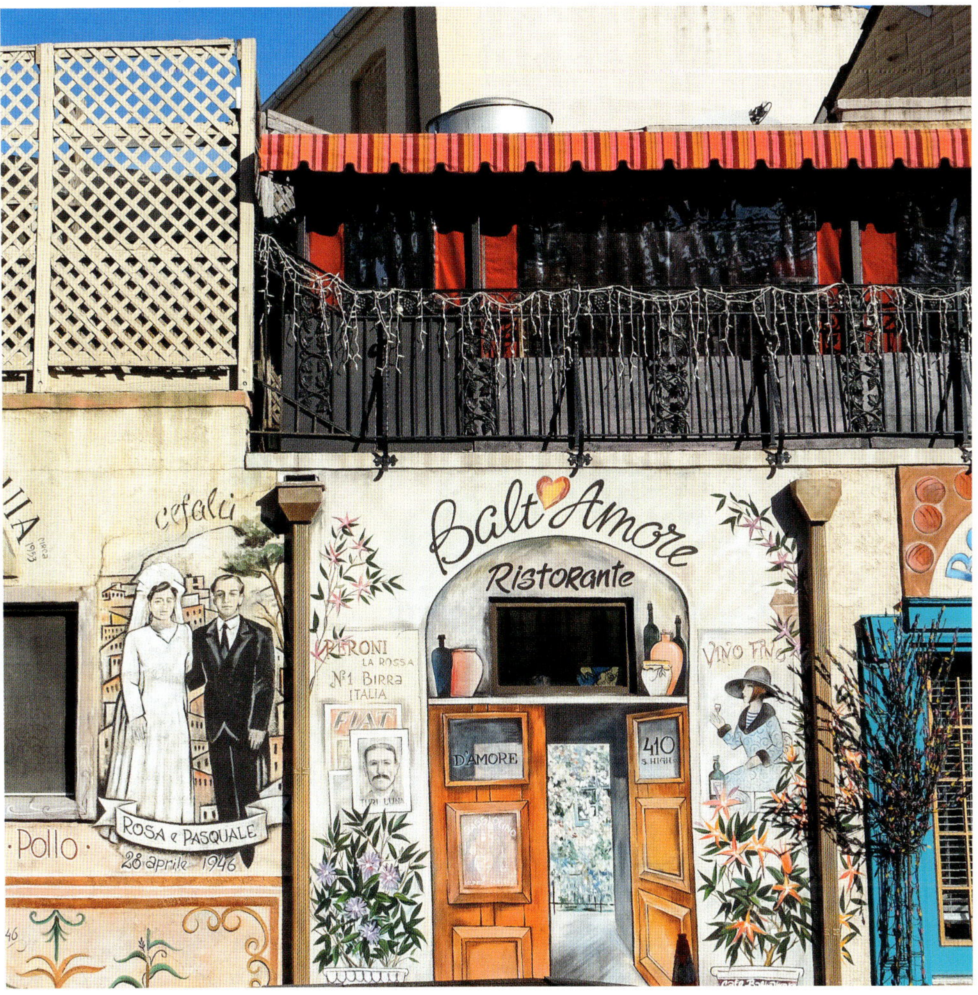

Little Italy

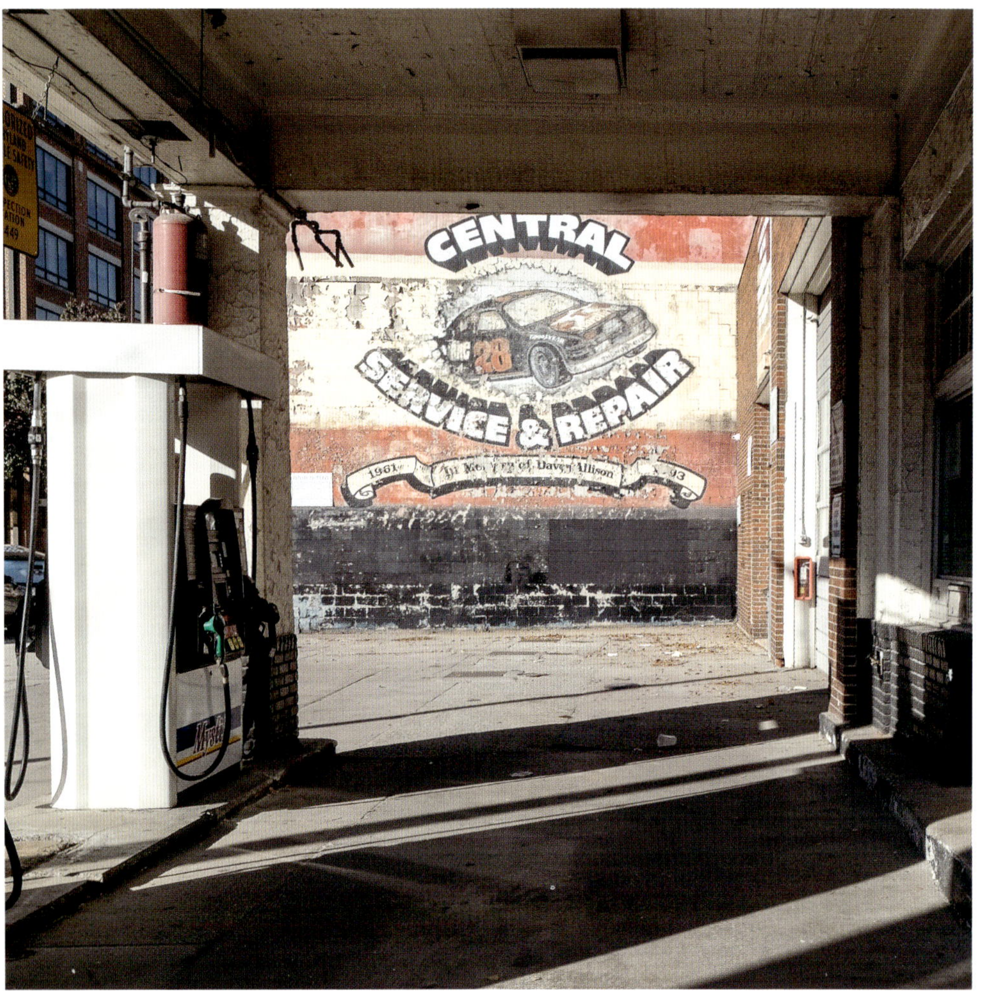

Little Italy

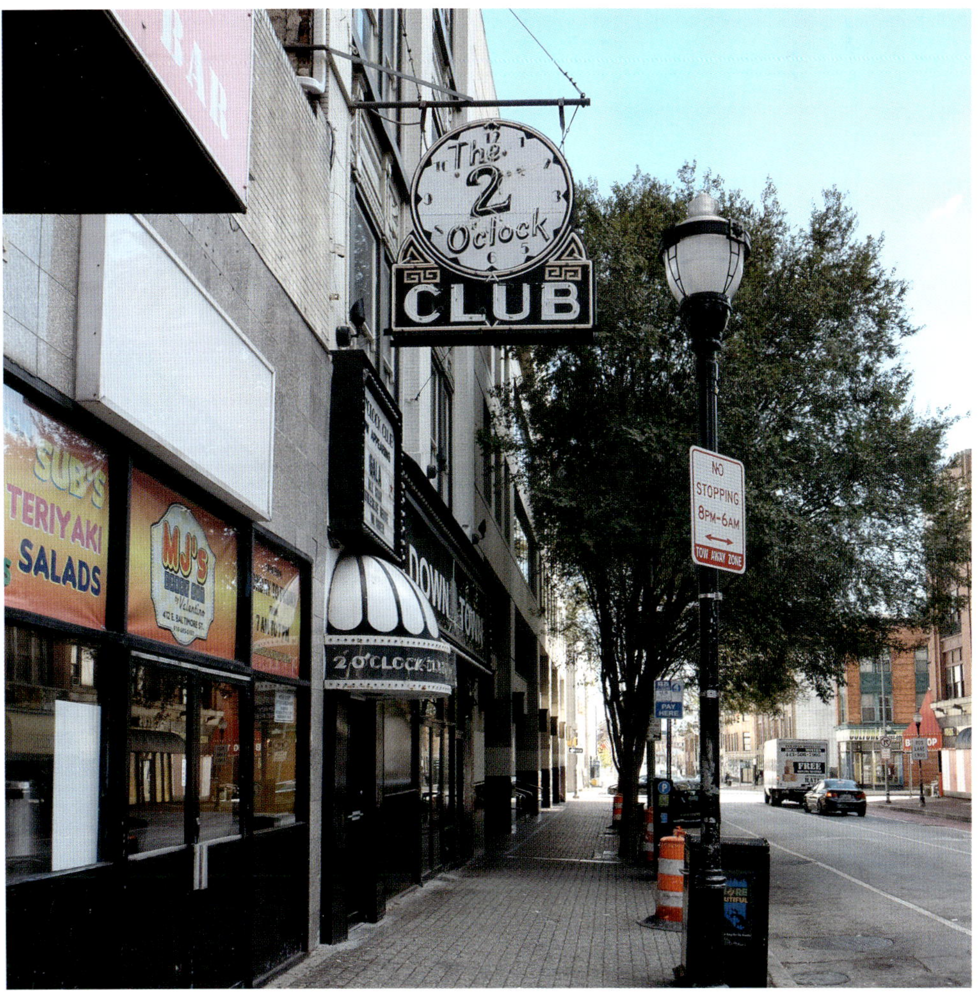

Baltimore Street

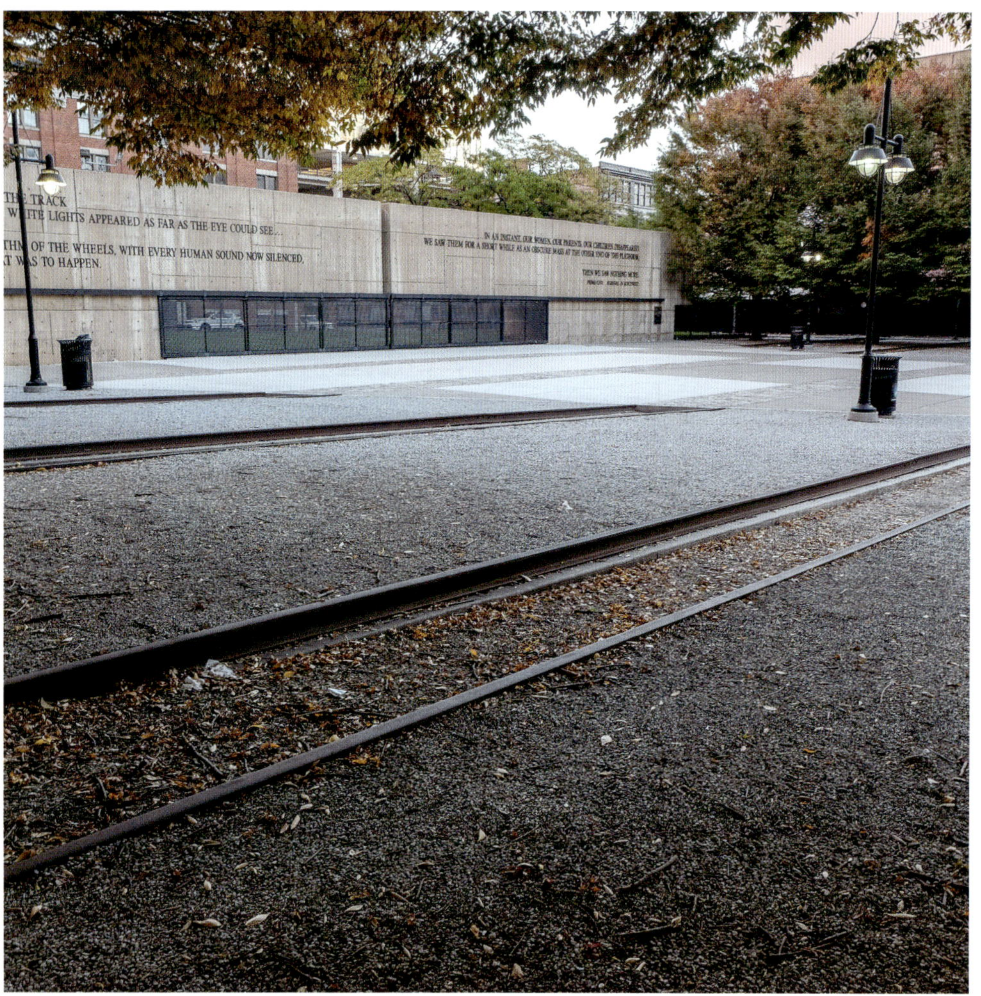

Holocaust Memorial Park

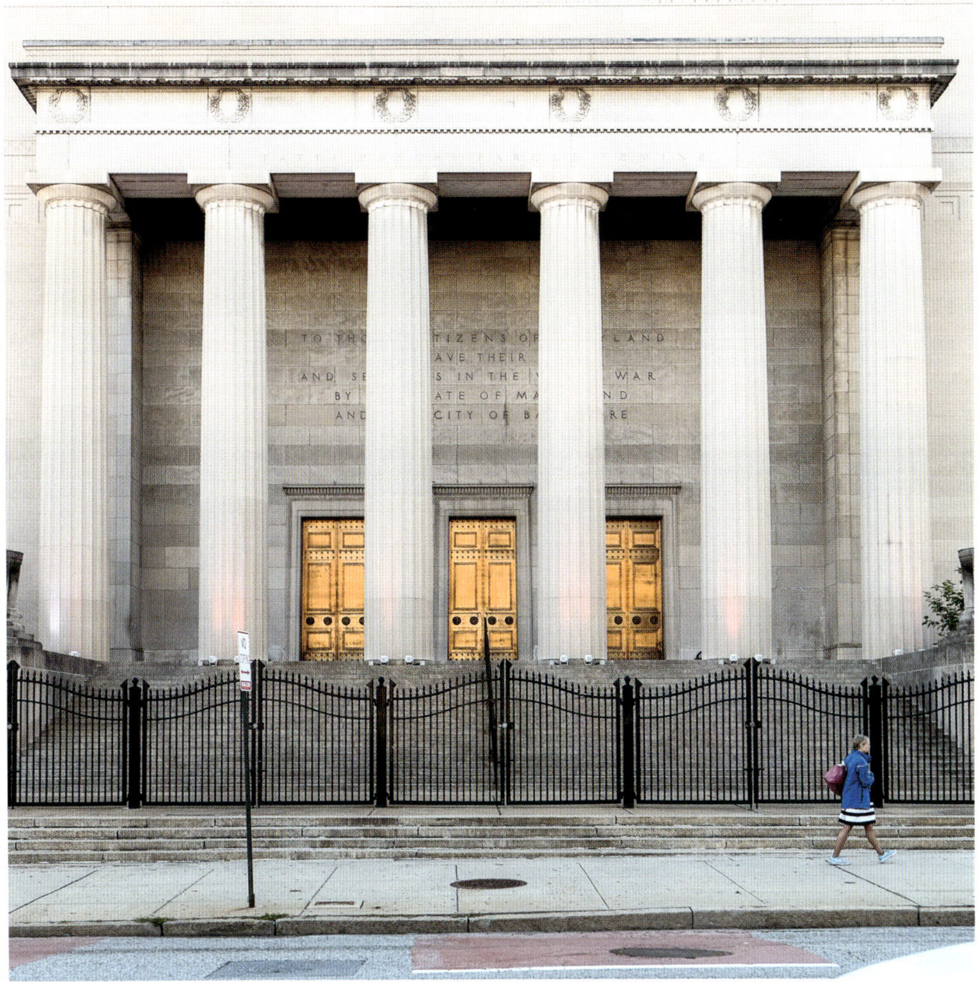

Baltimore War Memorial

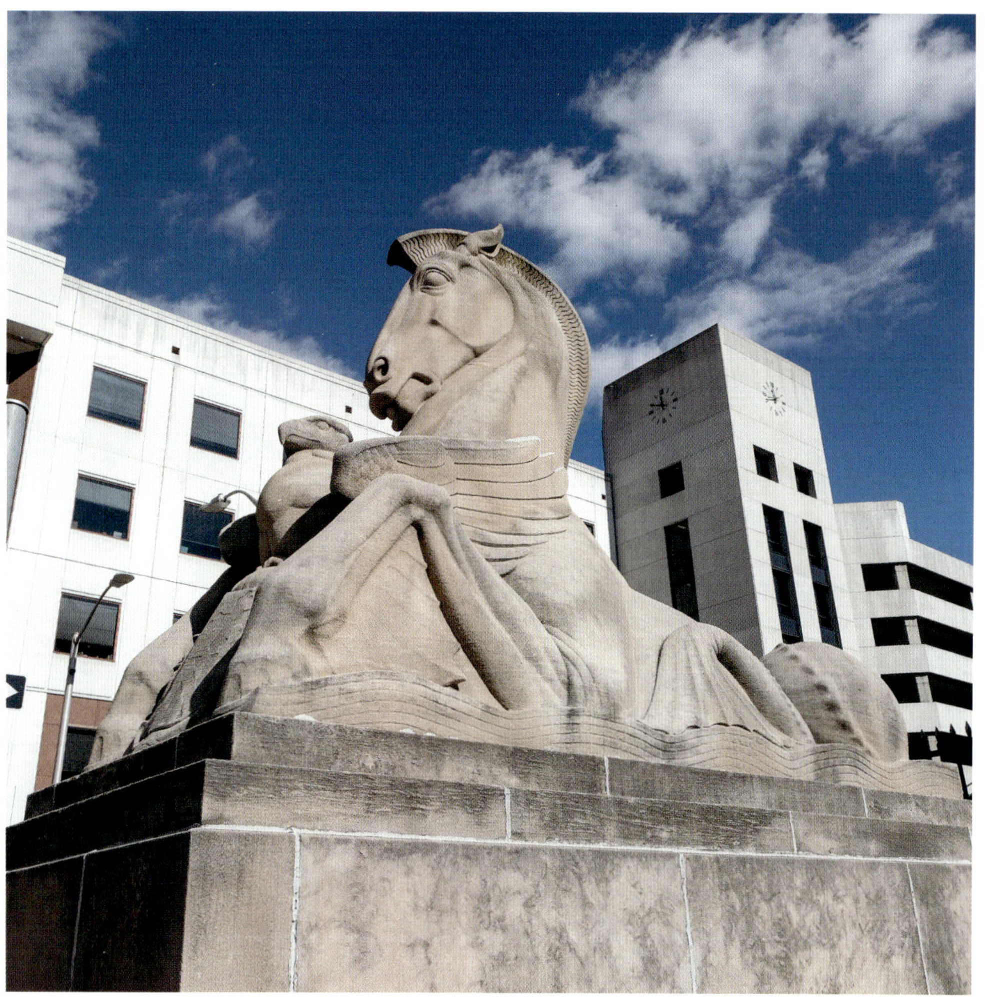

Baltimore War Memorial

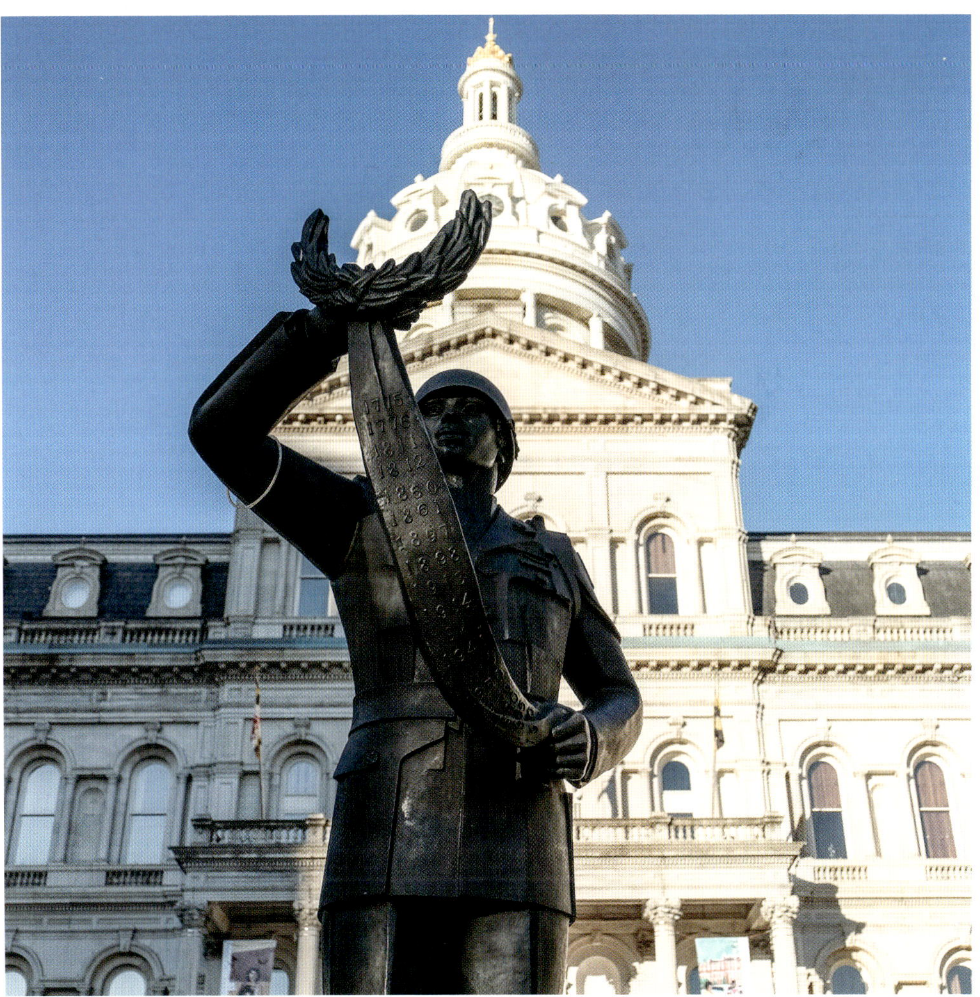

Baltimore City Hall and Black Soldier Memorial Statue

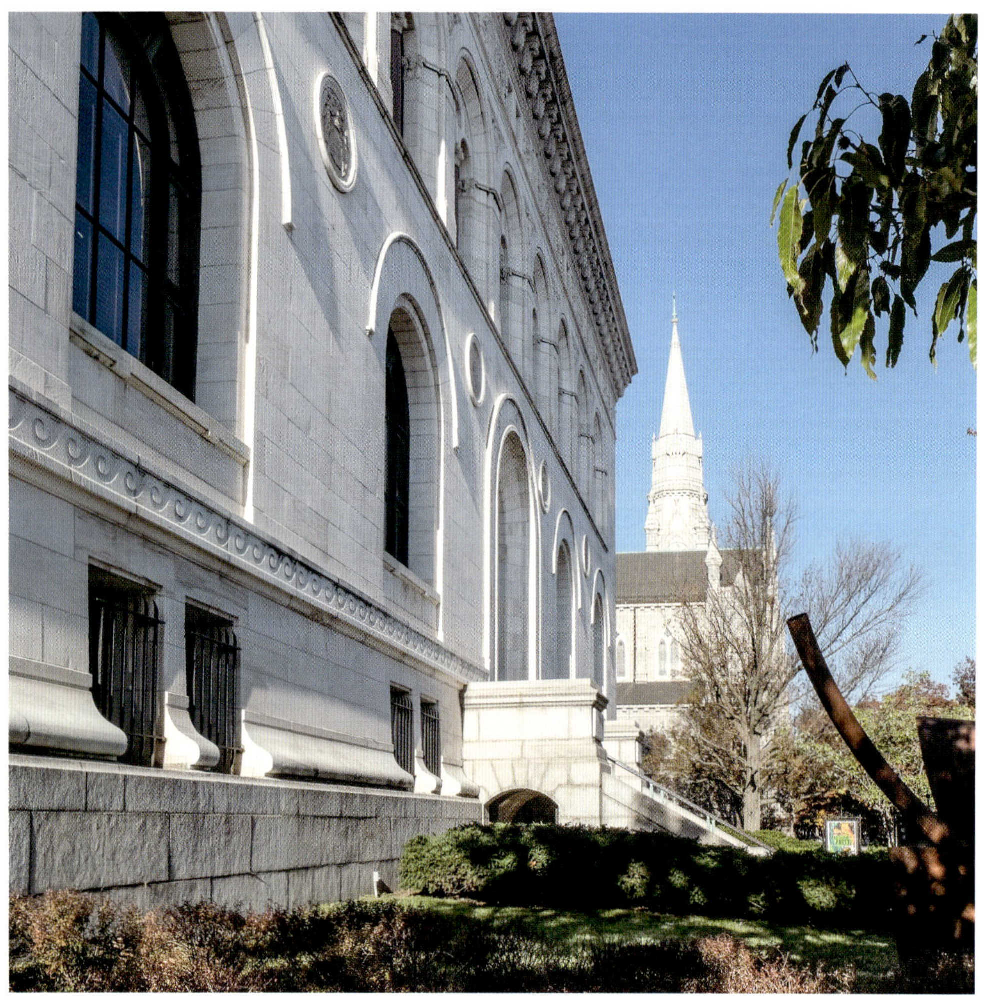

Maryland Institute College of Art, Bolton Hill

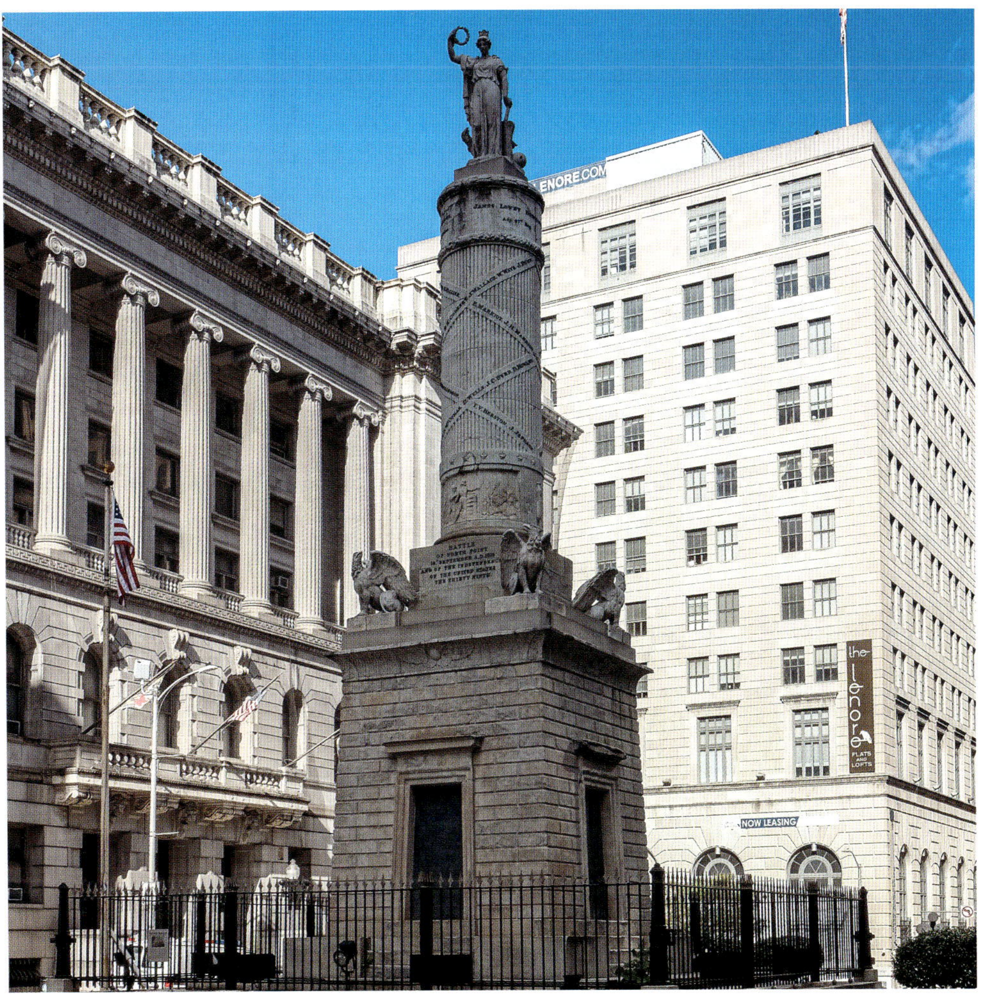

Battle Monument Square

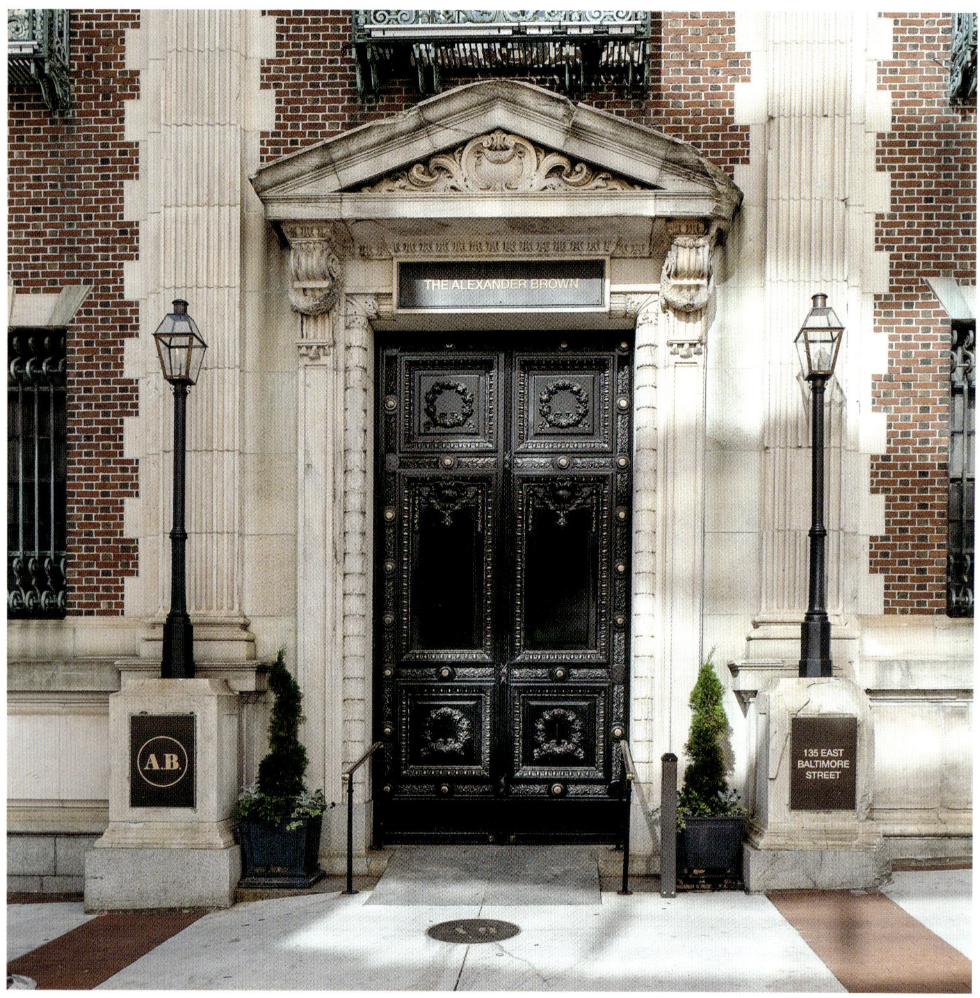

The Alexander Brown Restaurant, Baltimore Street

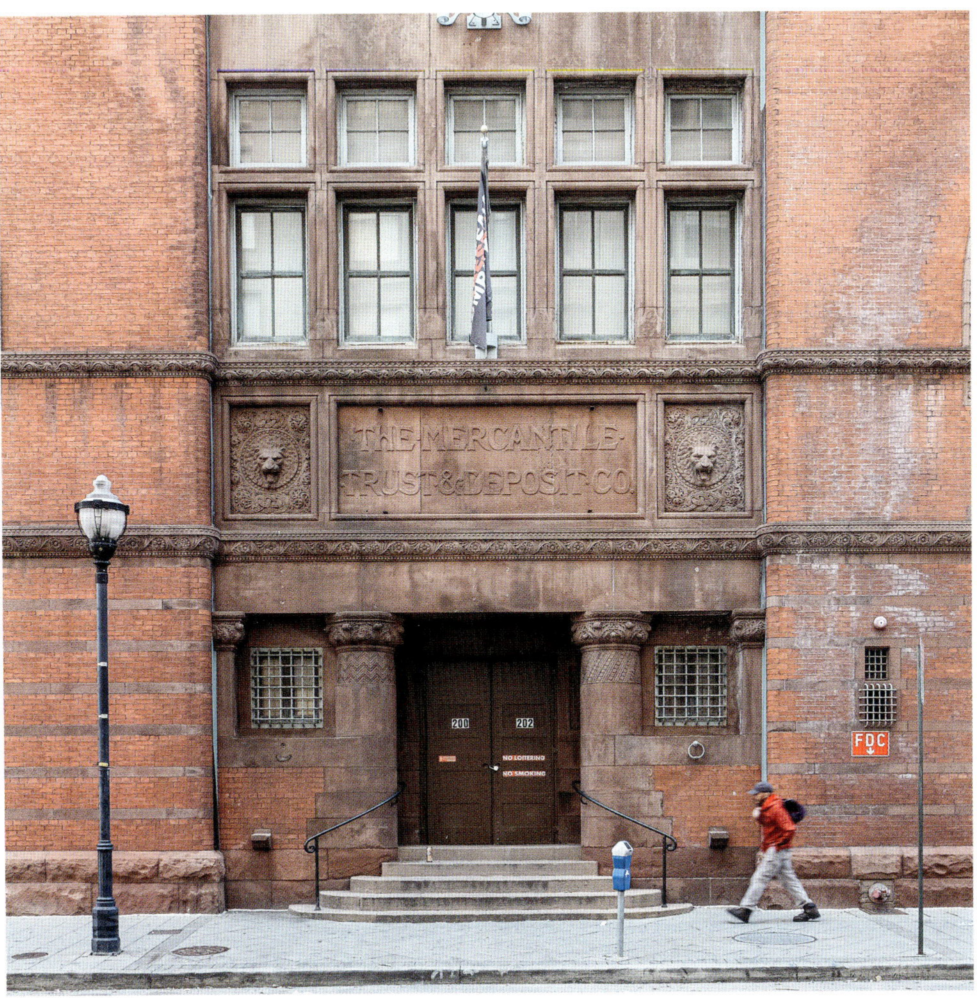

Redwood Street

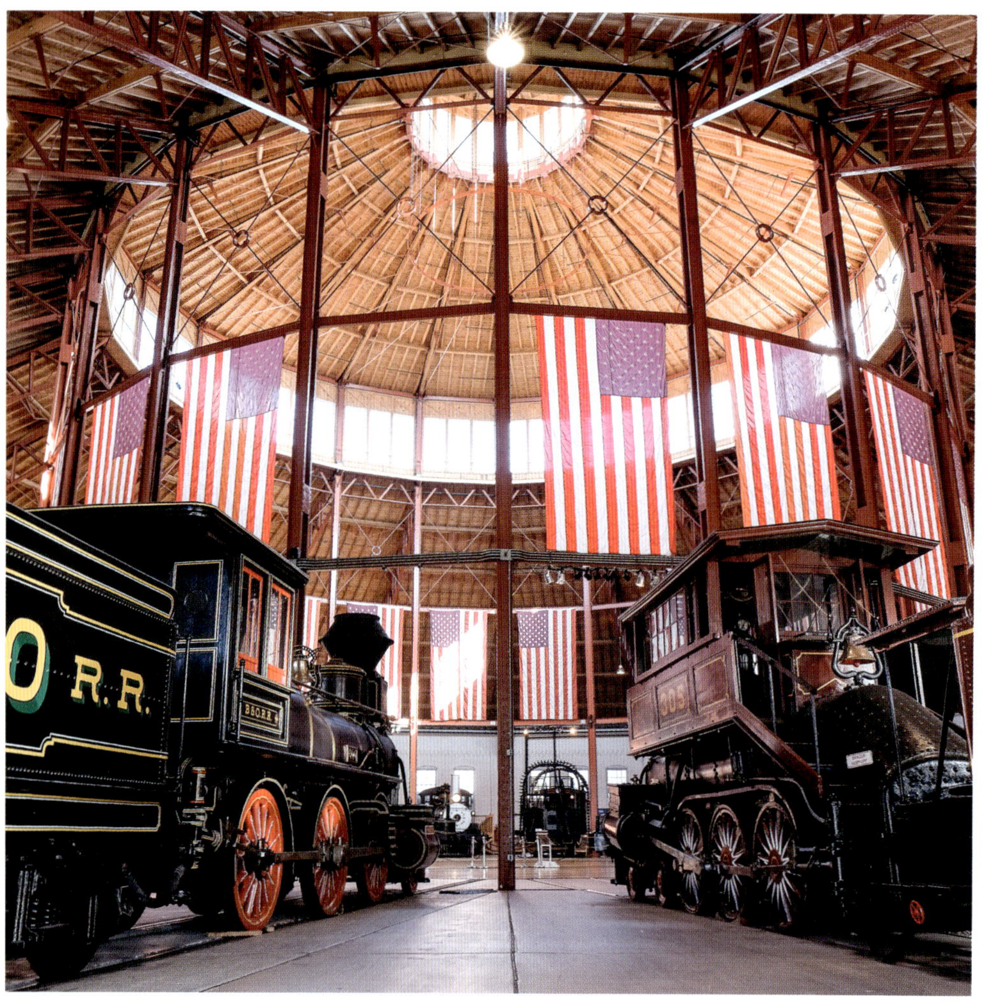

B&O Railroad Museum

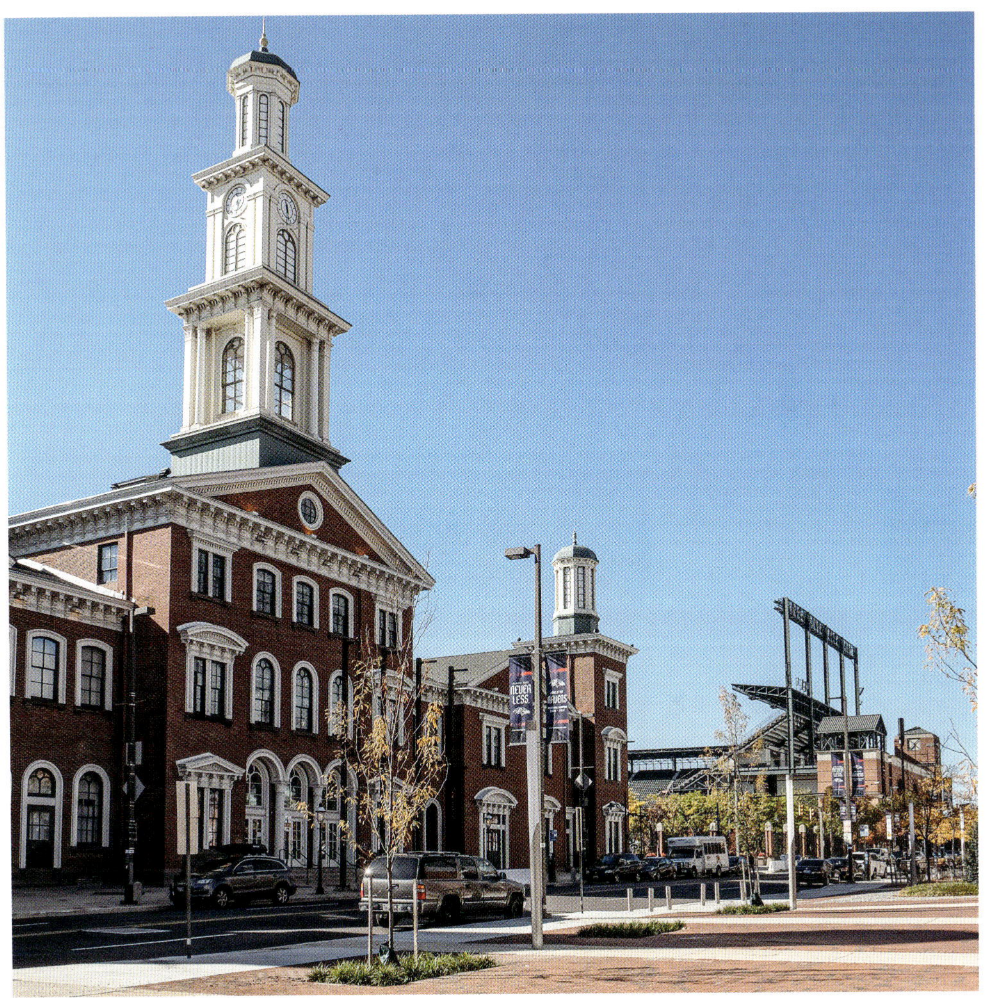

Camden Yards Railroad Station

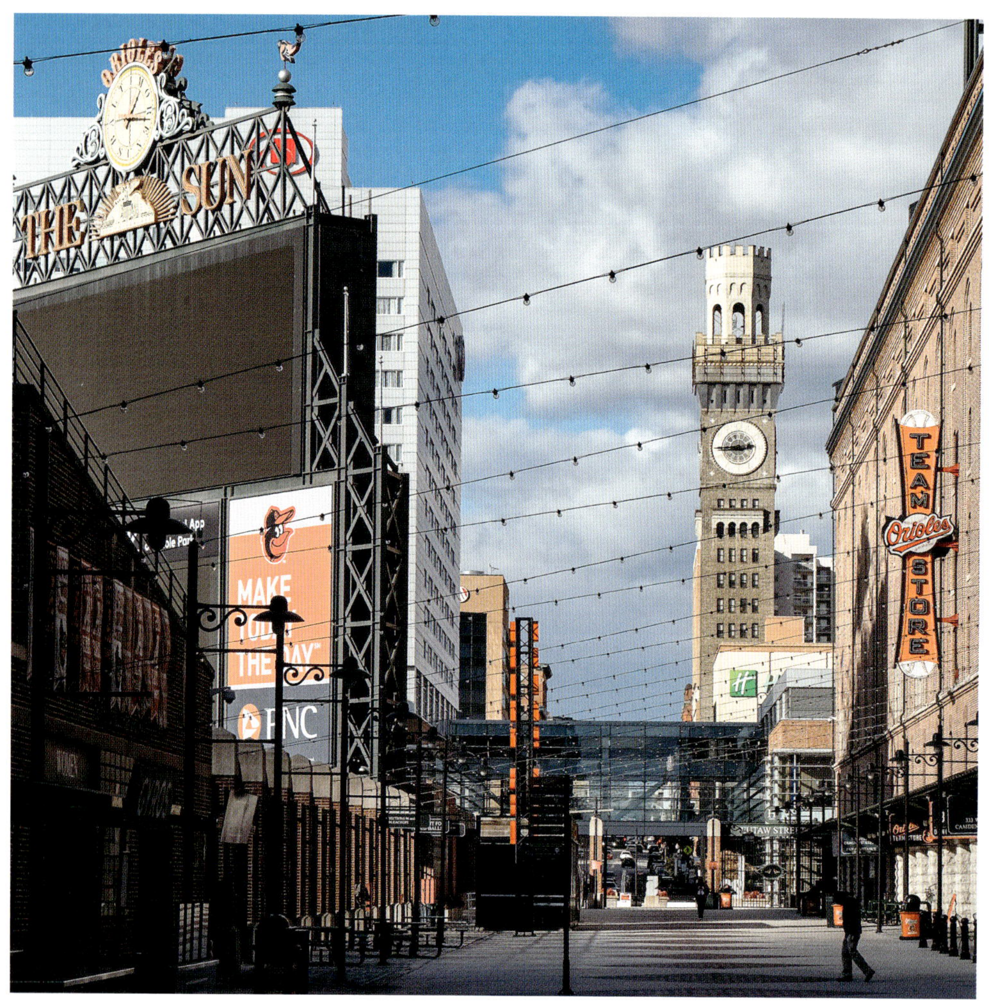

Oriole Park at Camden Yards, Bromo-Seltzer Arts Tower in background

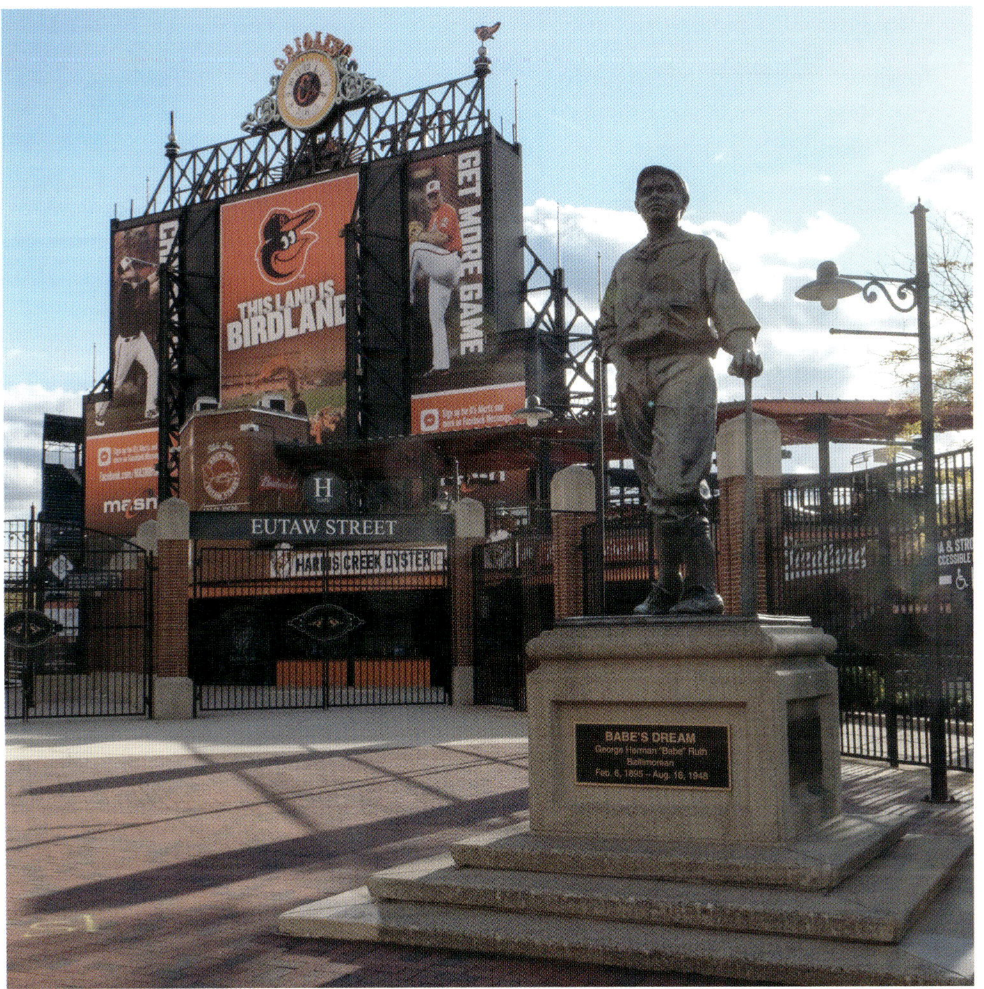

Oriole Park at Camden Yards

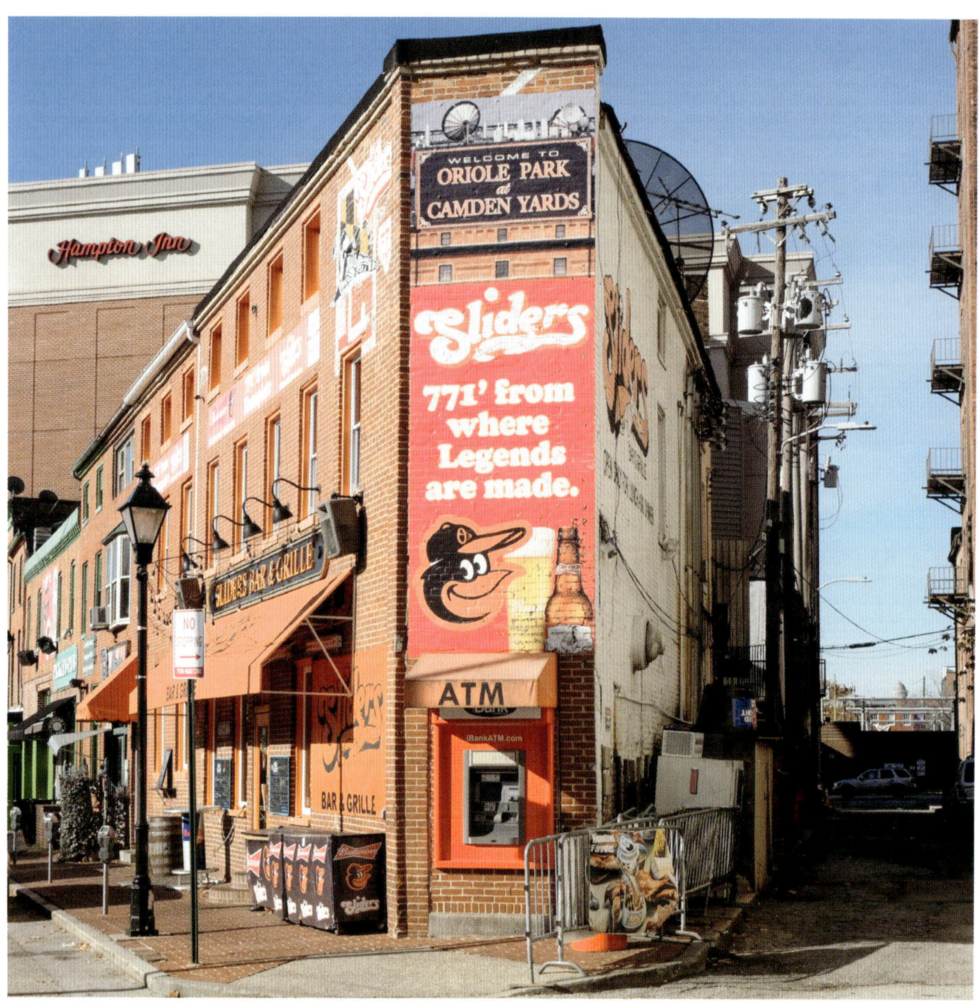

Washington Boulevard

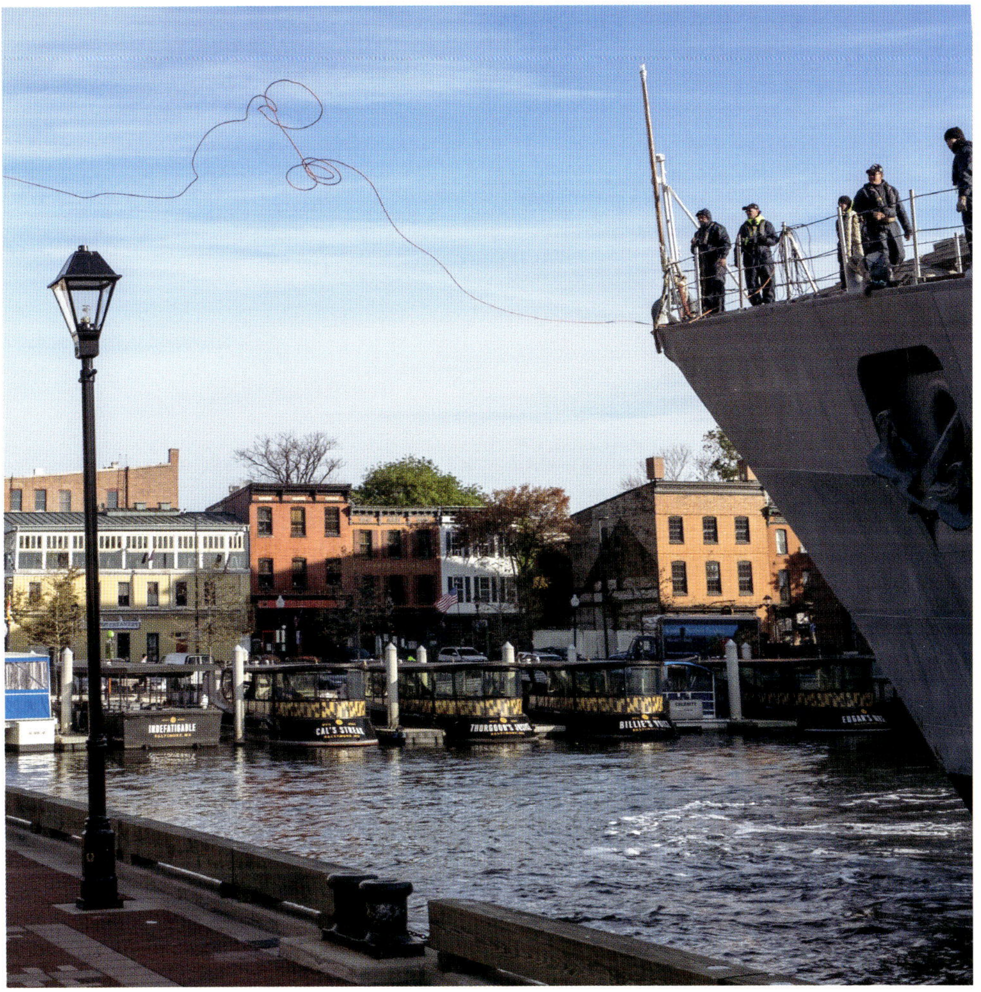

Fells Point

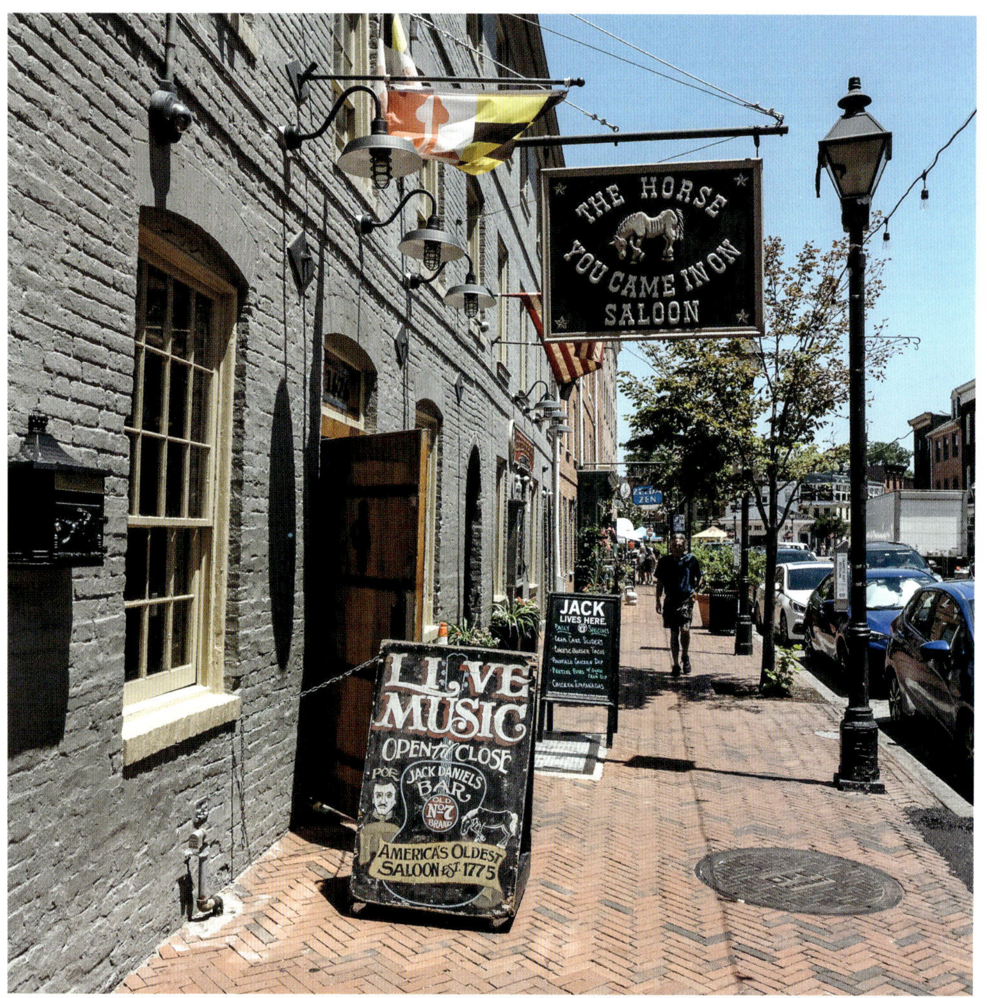

Thames Street, Fells Point

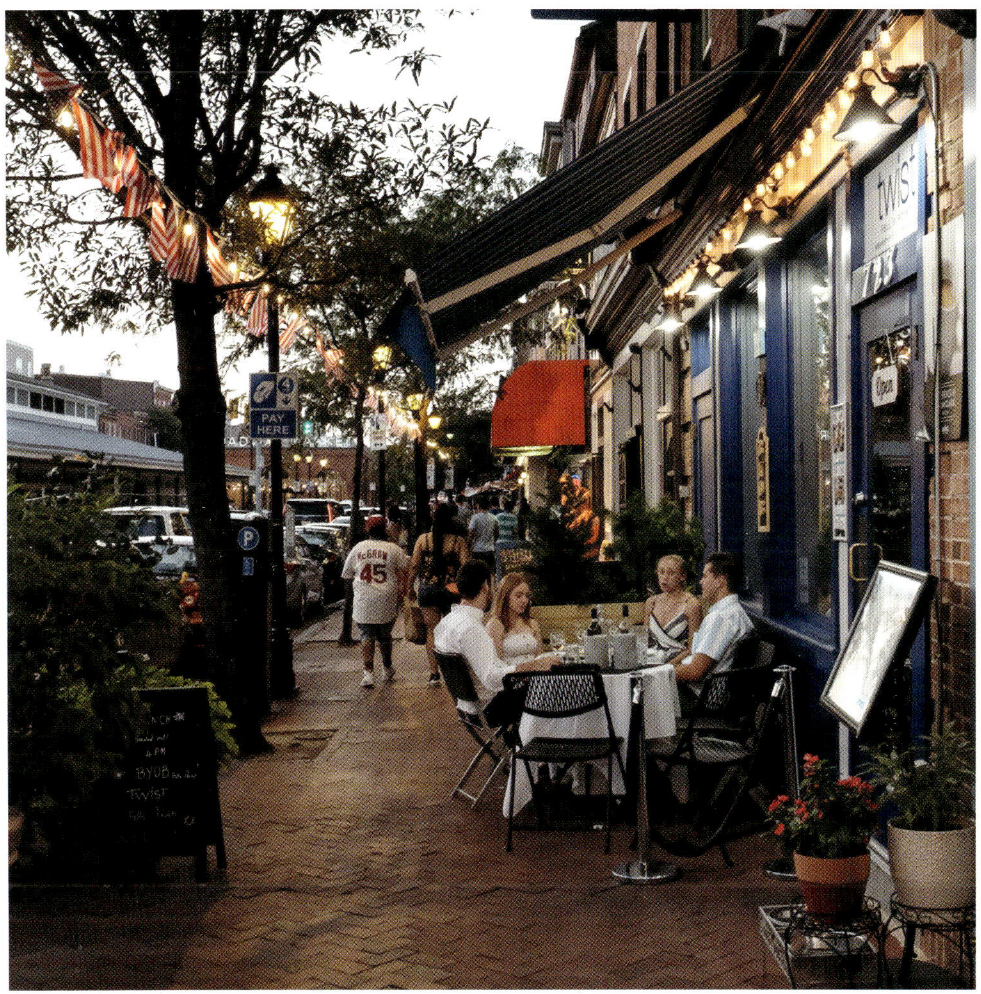

Broadway Square, Fells Point

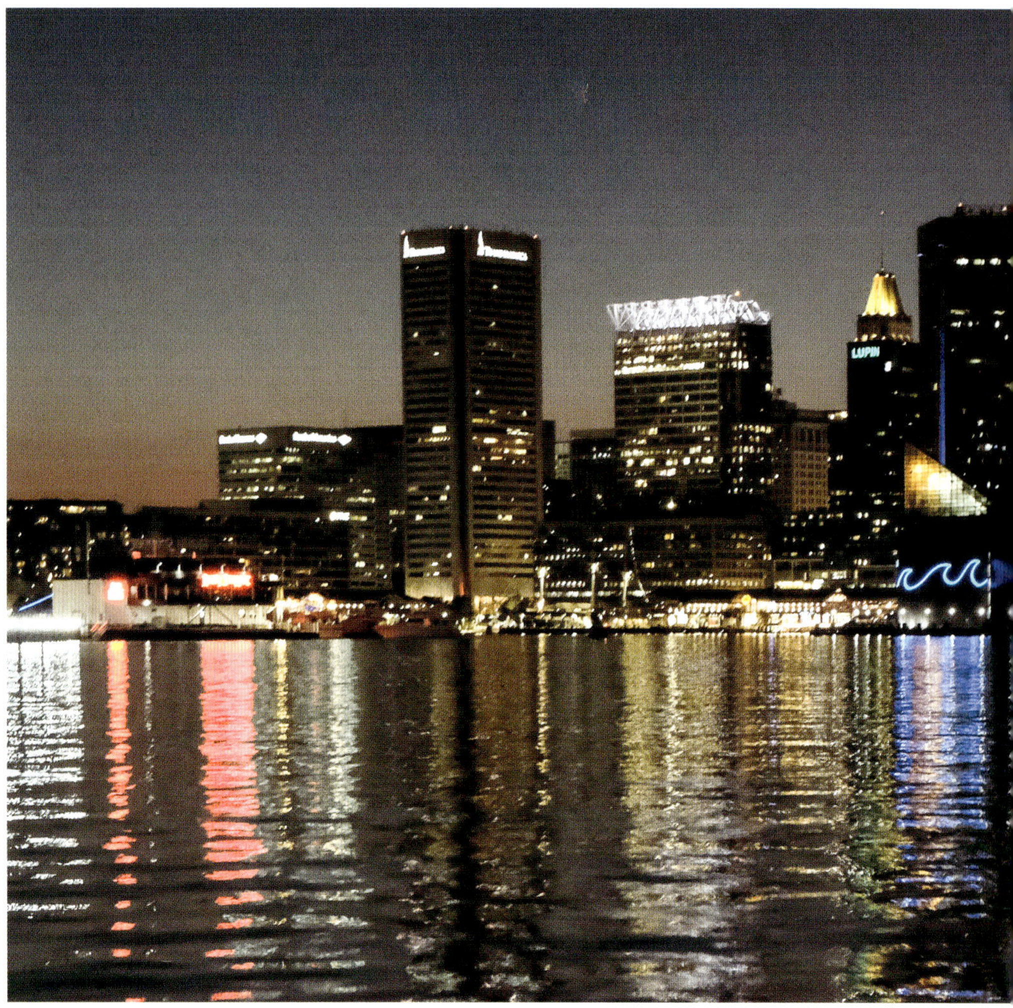

Inner Harbor

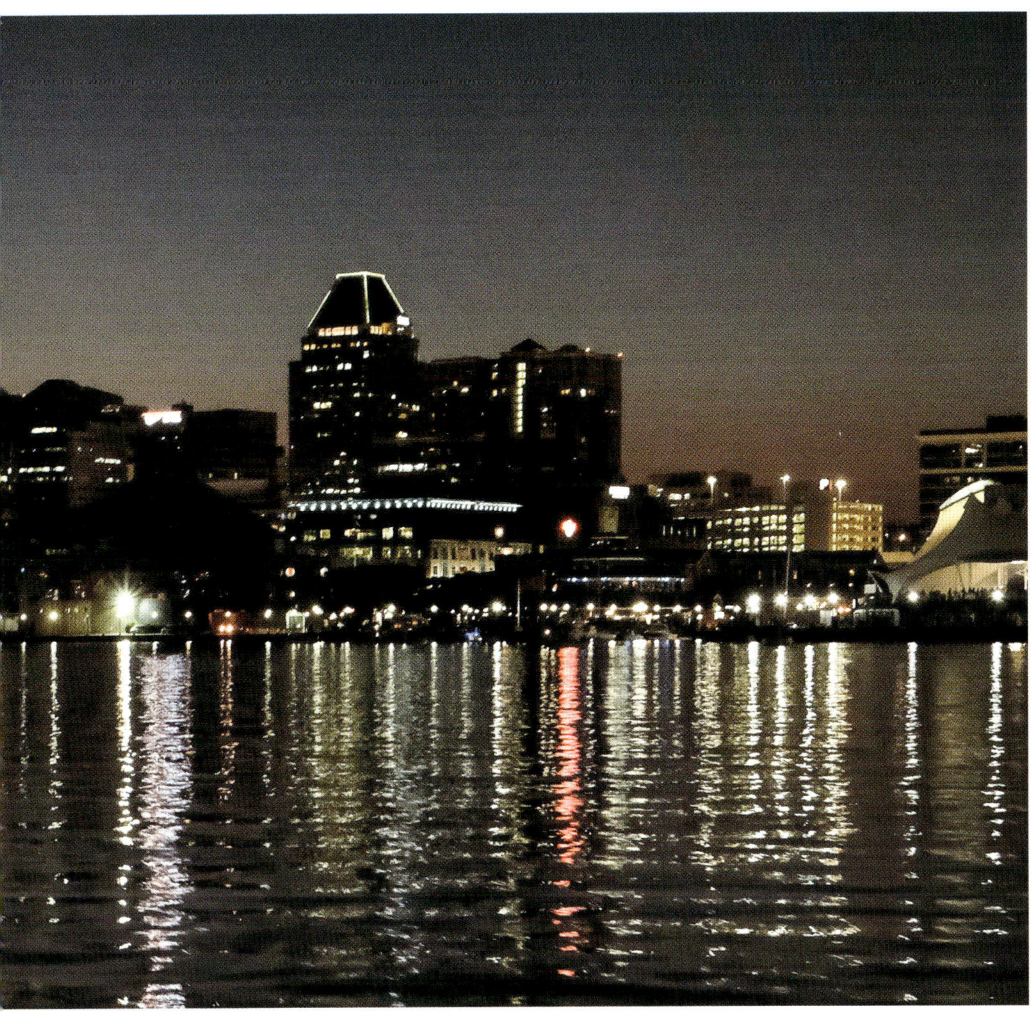

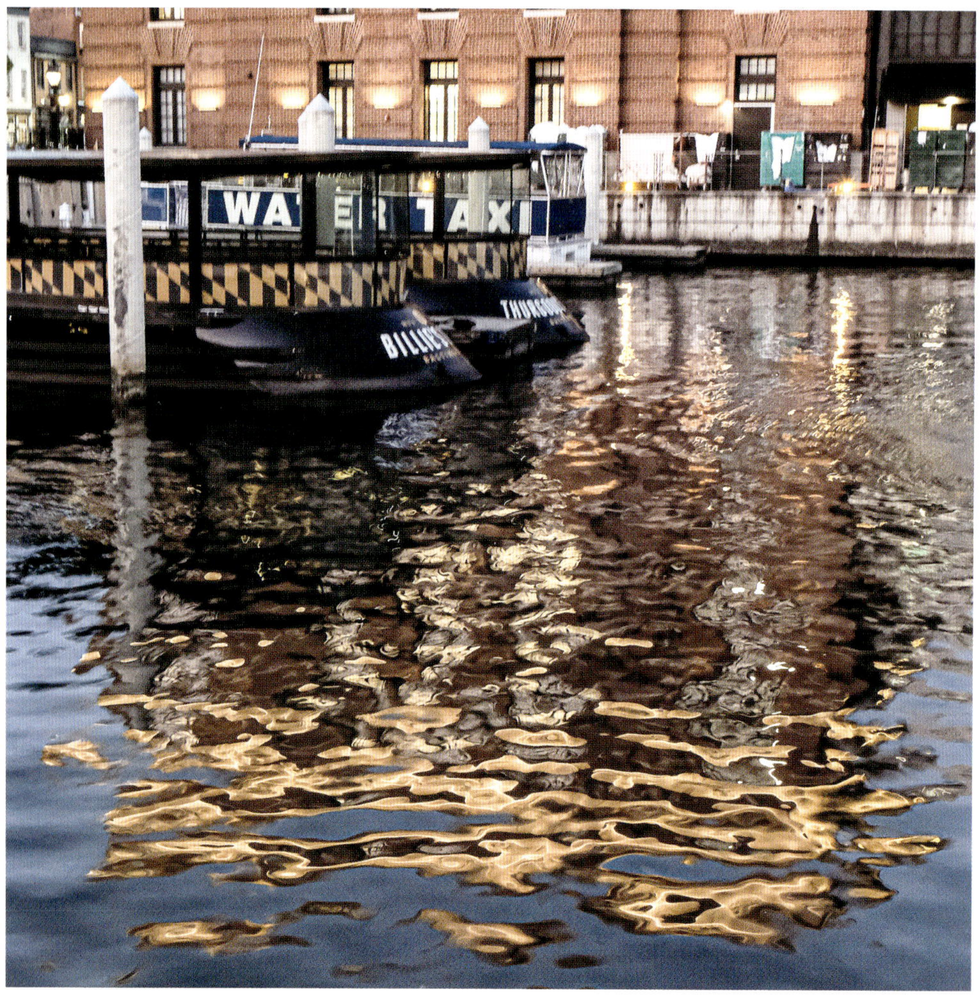

Fells Point

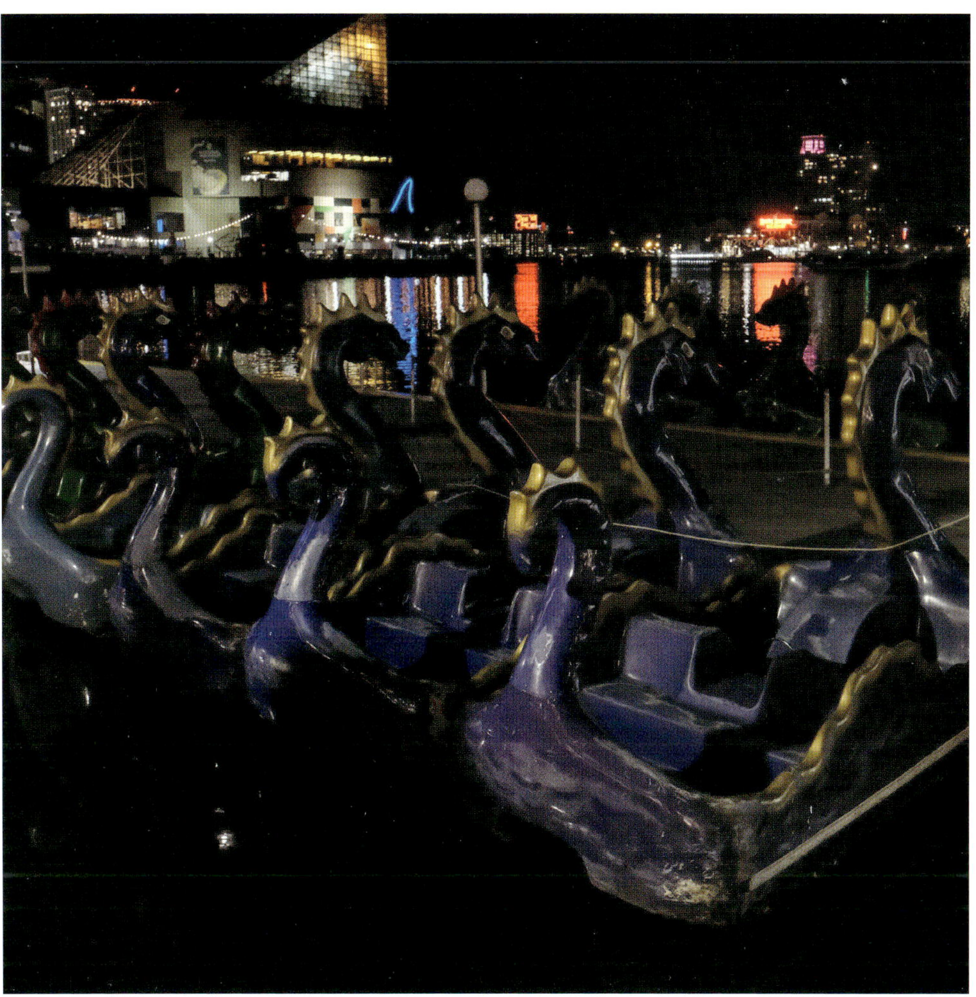

Inner Harbor

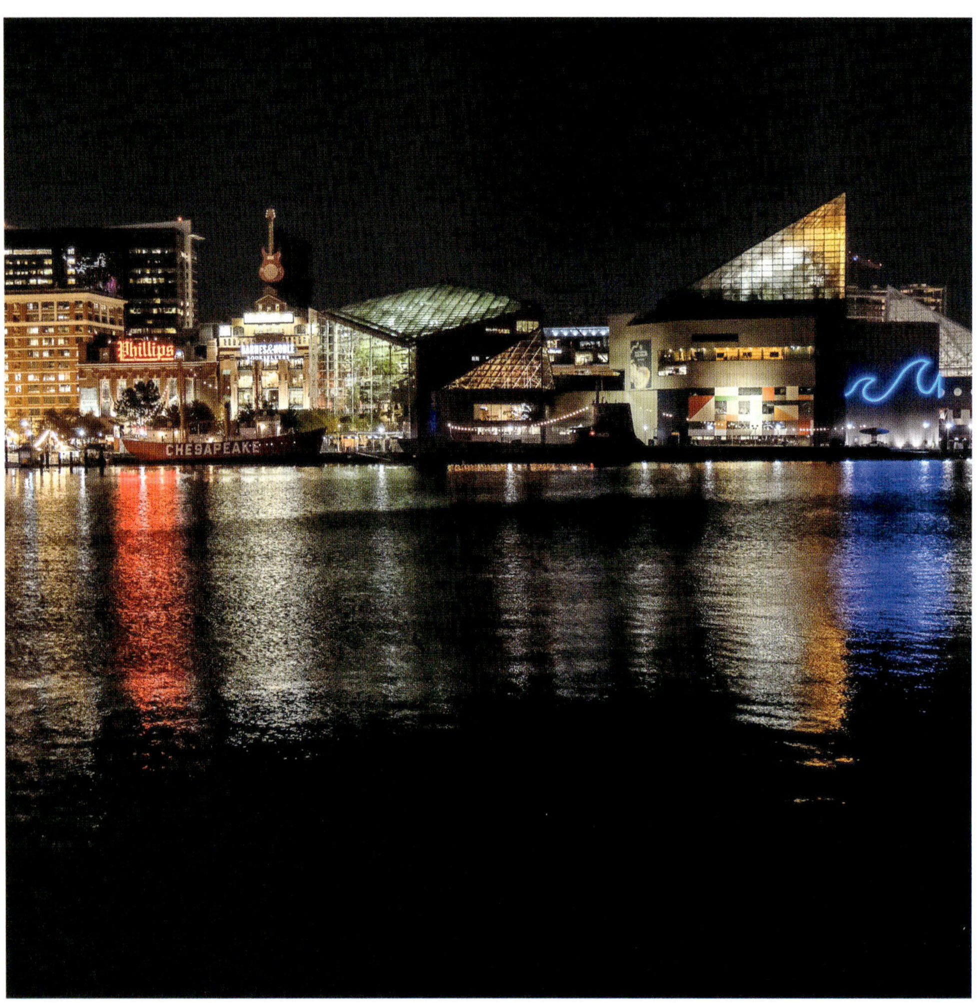

Inner Harbor

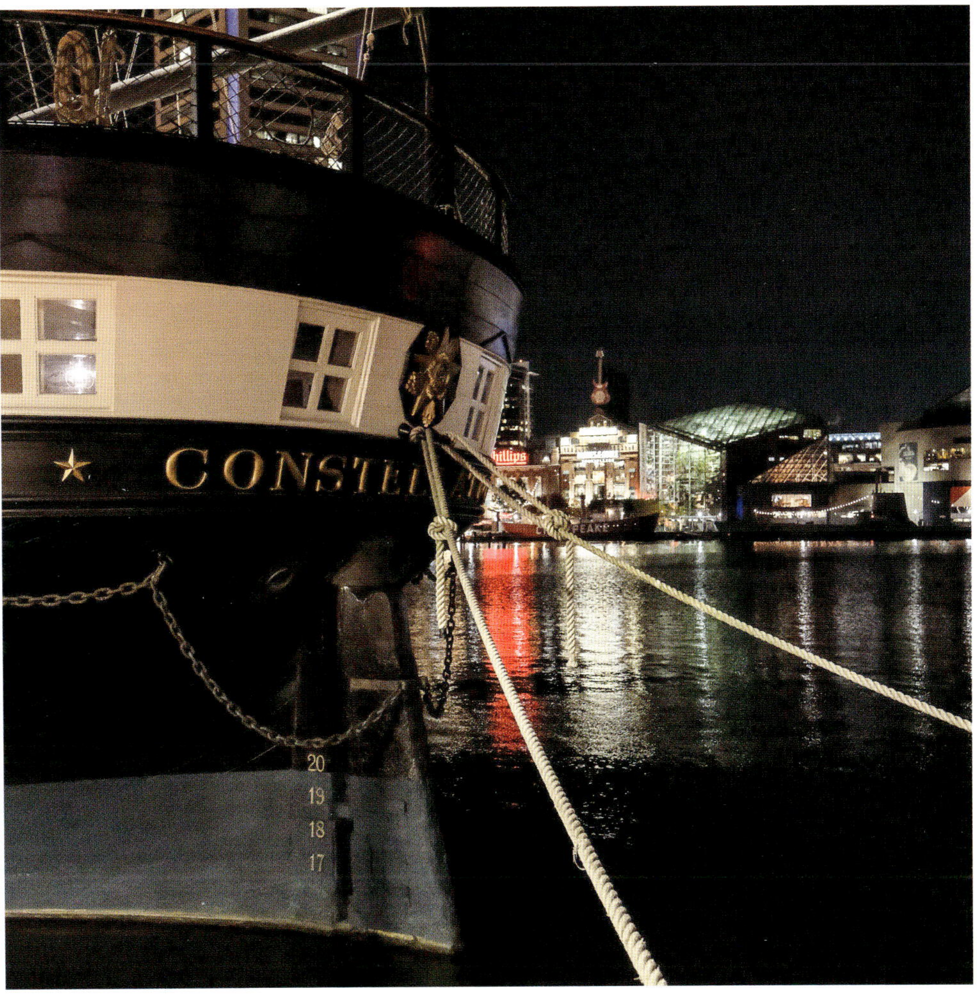

USS Constellation

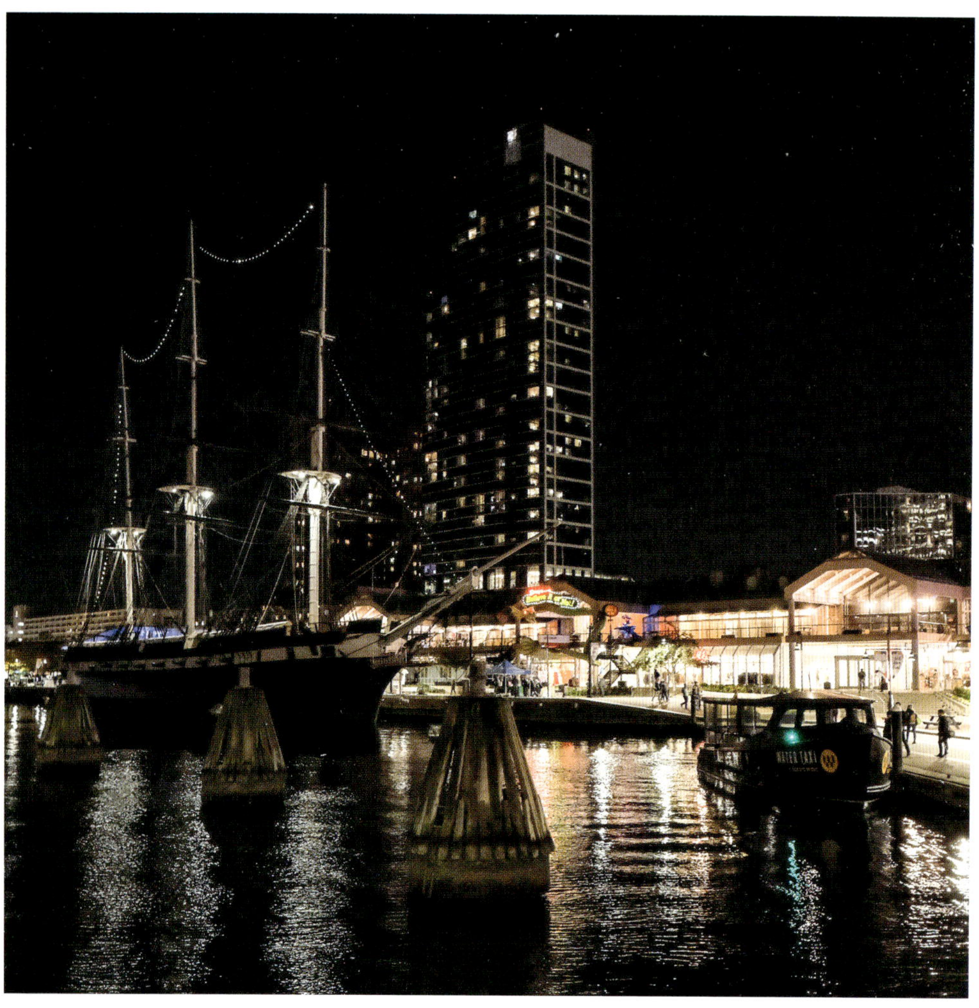

USS Constellation, *Harbor Place, Inner Harbor*

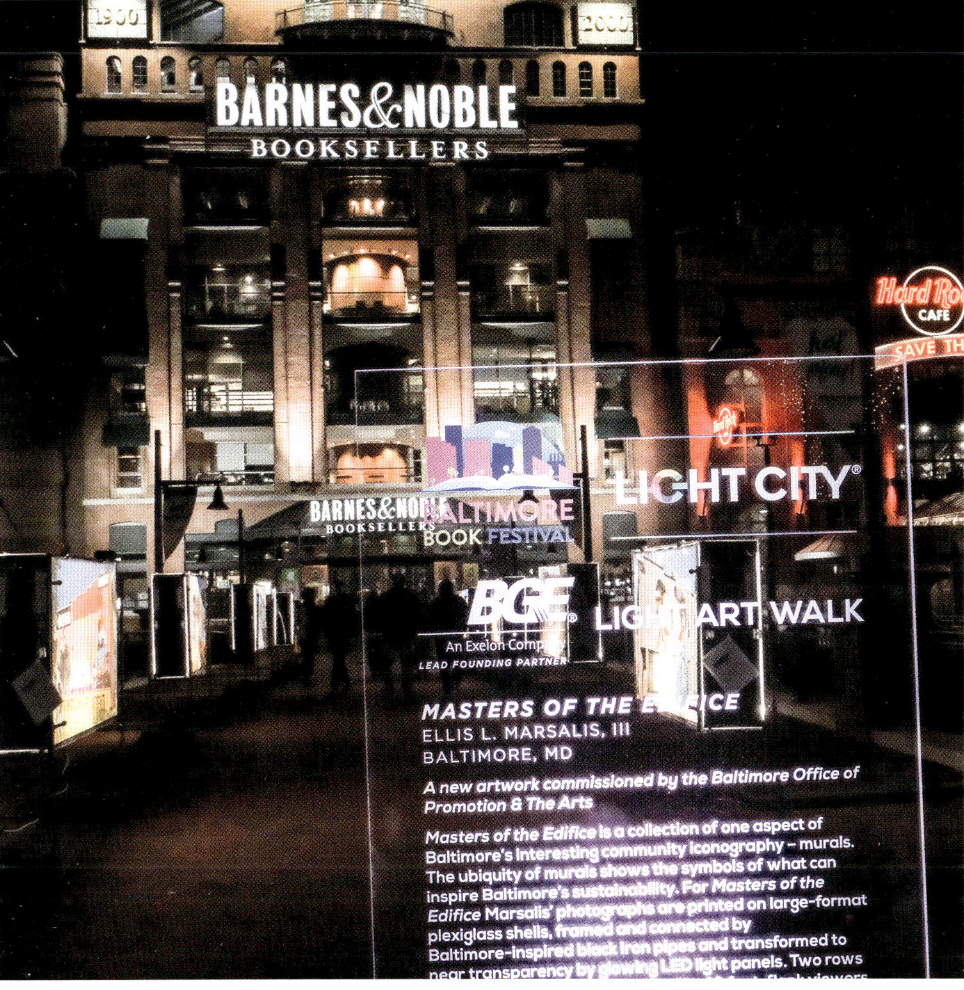

Inner Harbor

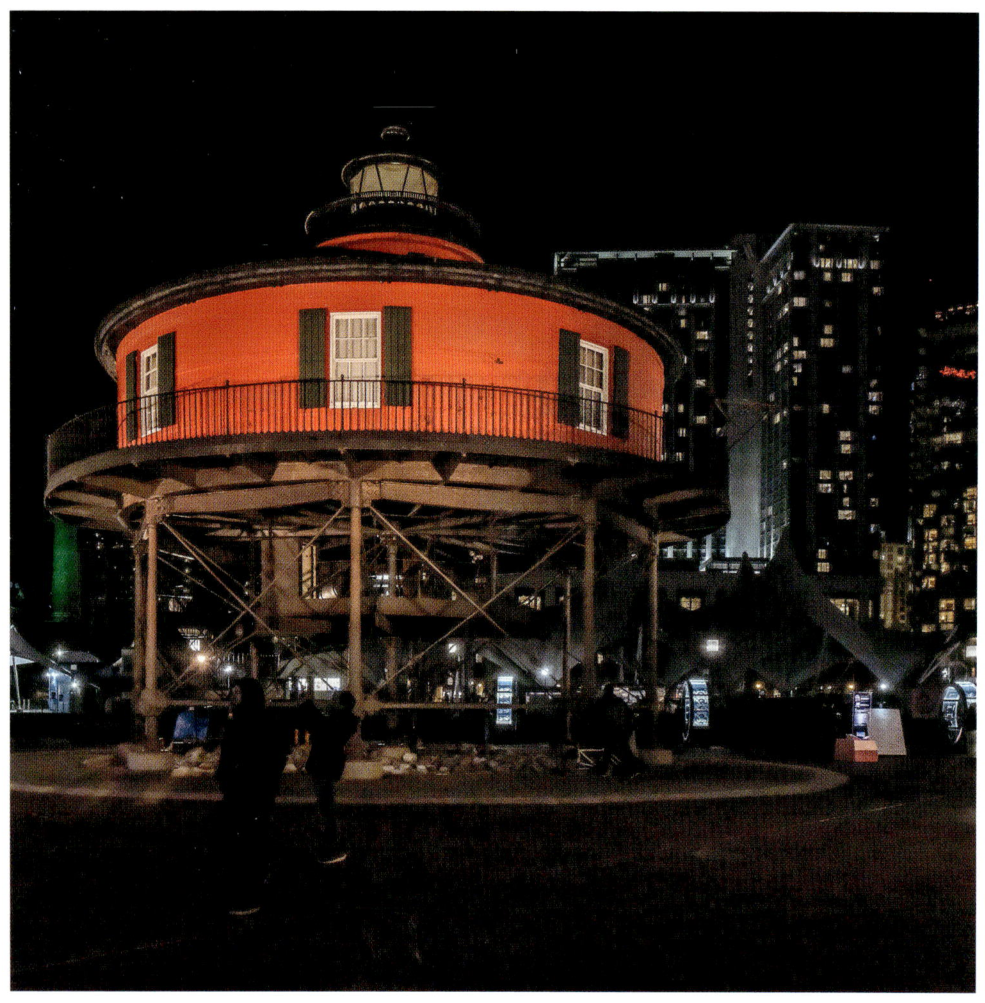

Screw-pile lighthouse, Inner Harbor

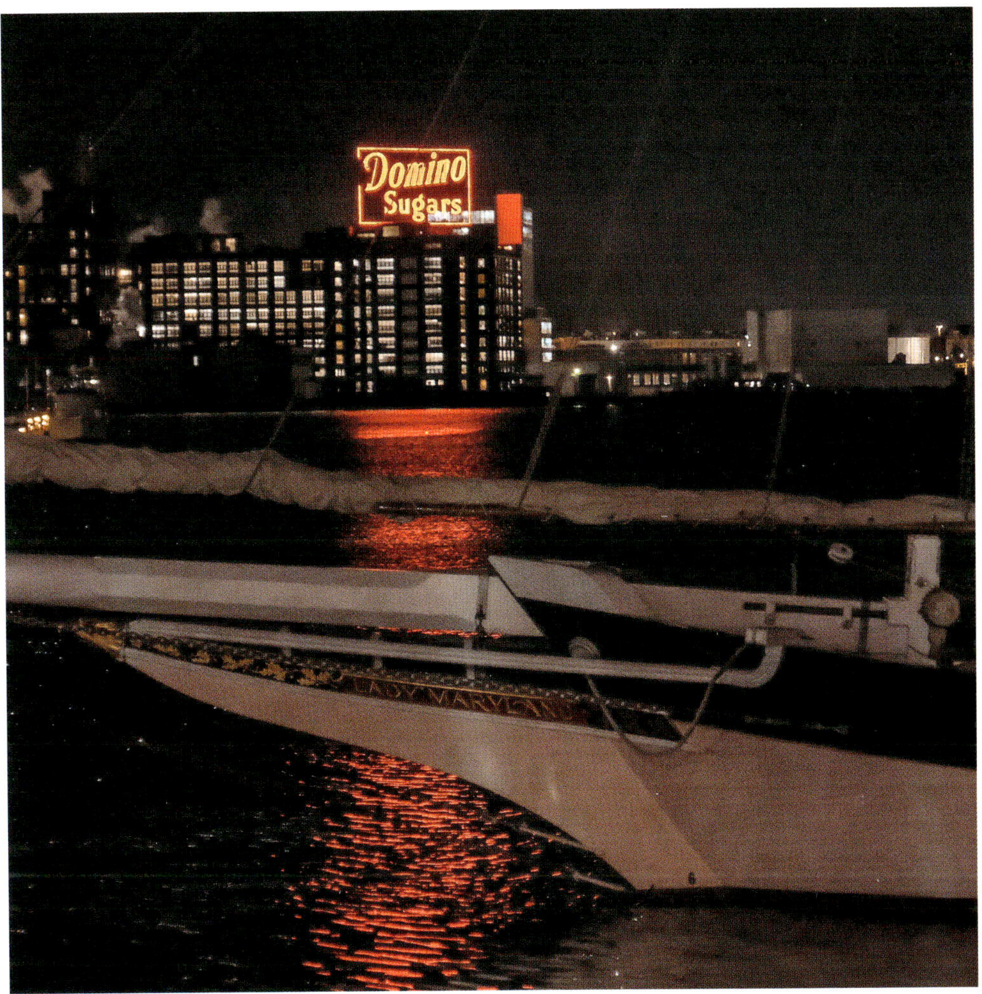

Domino Sugar Building

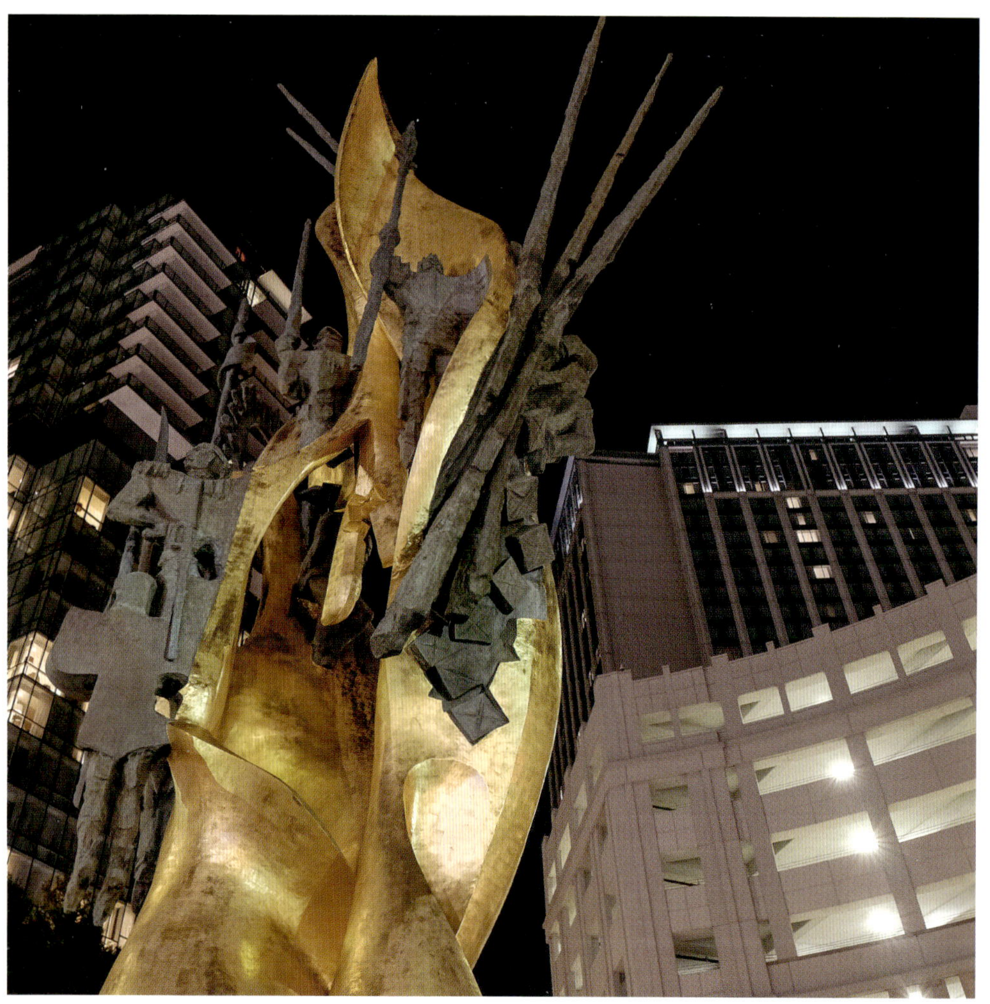

National Katyń Memorial, Inner Harbor East

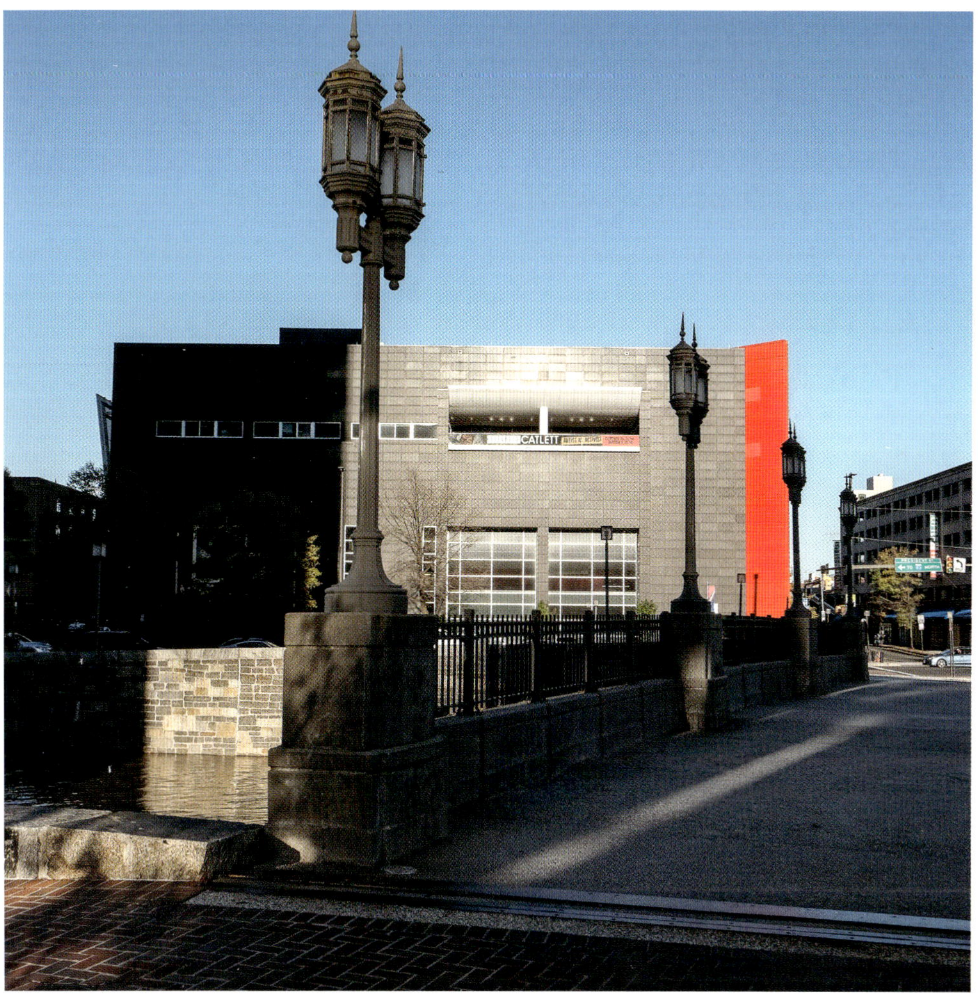

Reginald F. Lewis Museum

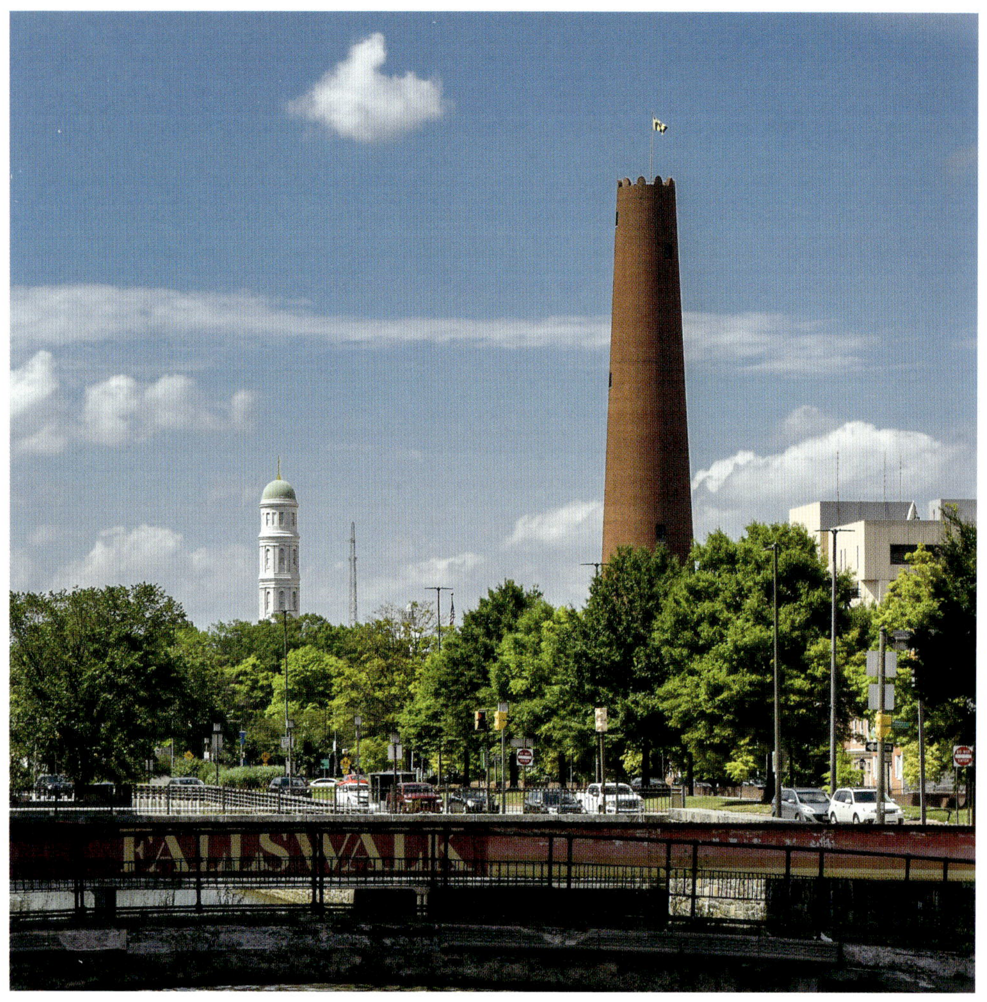

Patapsco River, Baltimore Phoenix Shot Tower

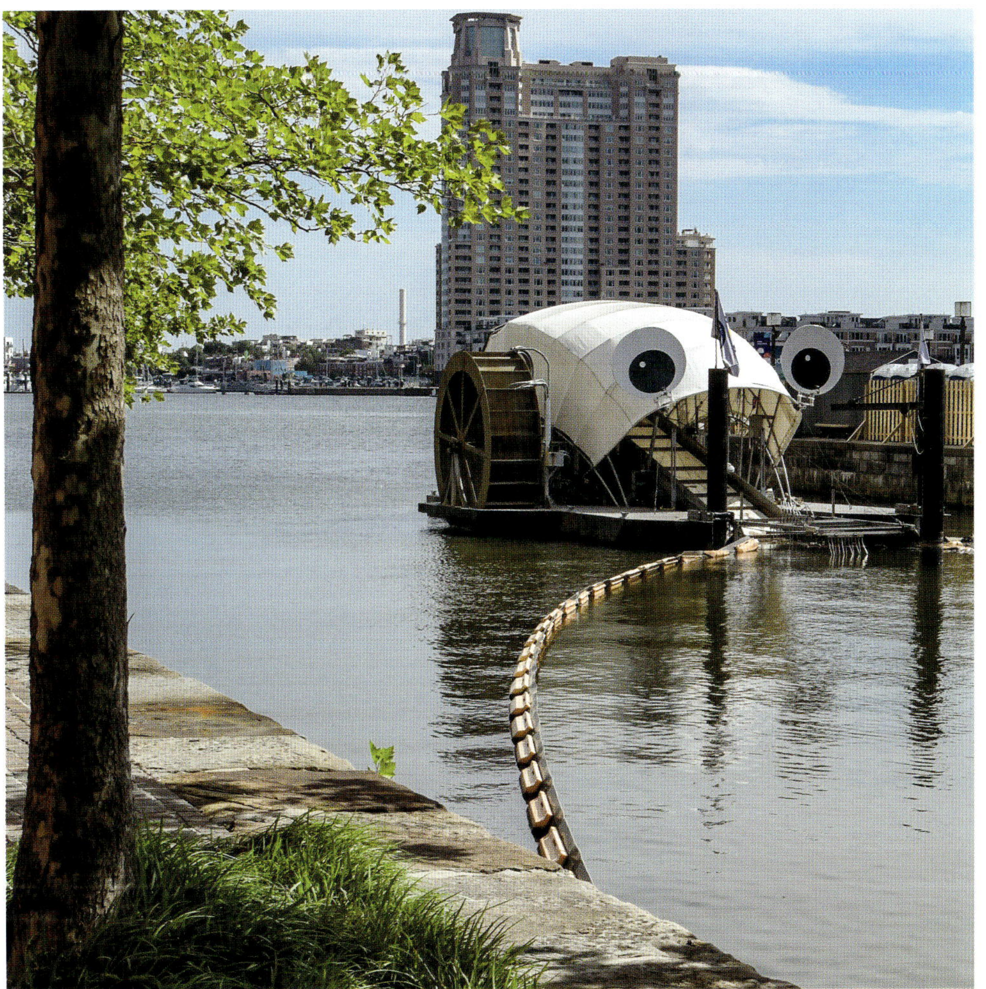

Patapsco River

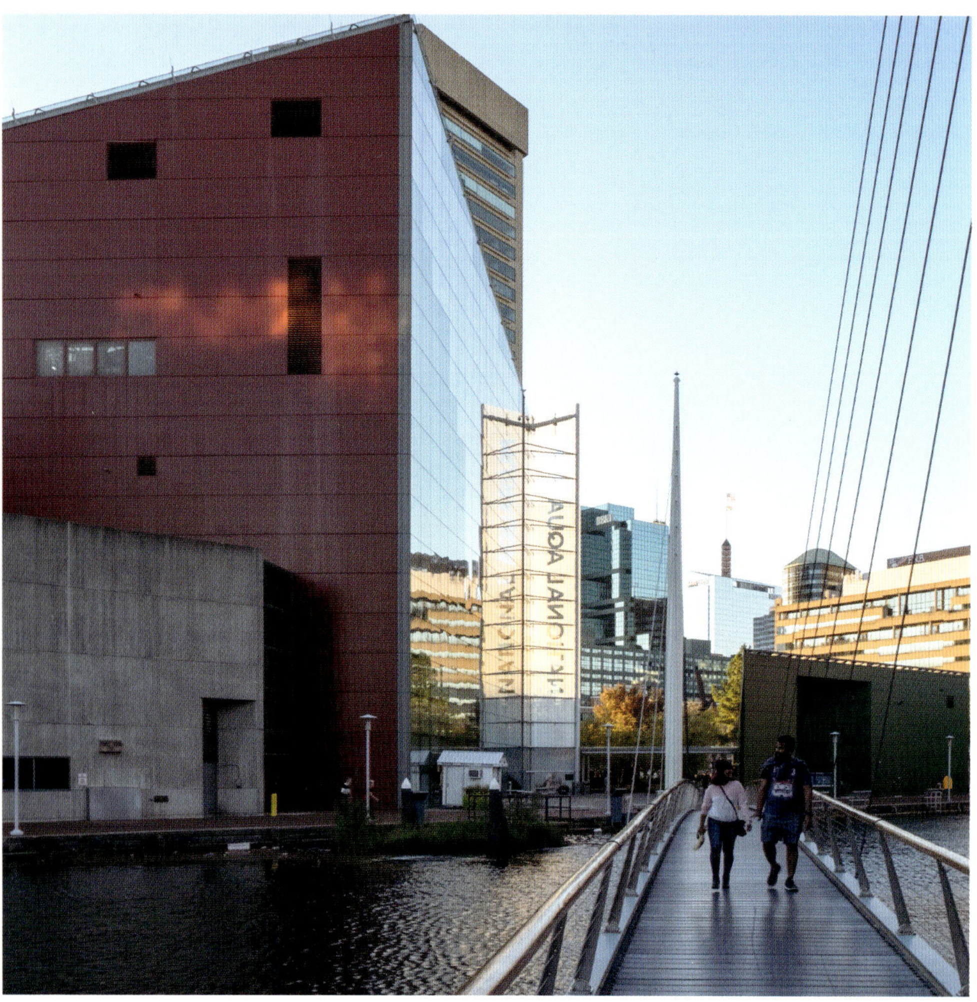

Inner Harbor

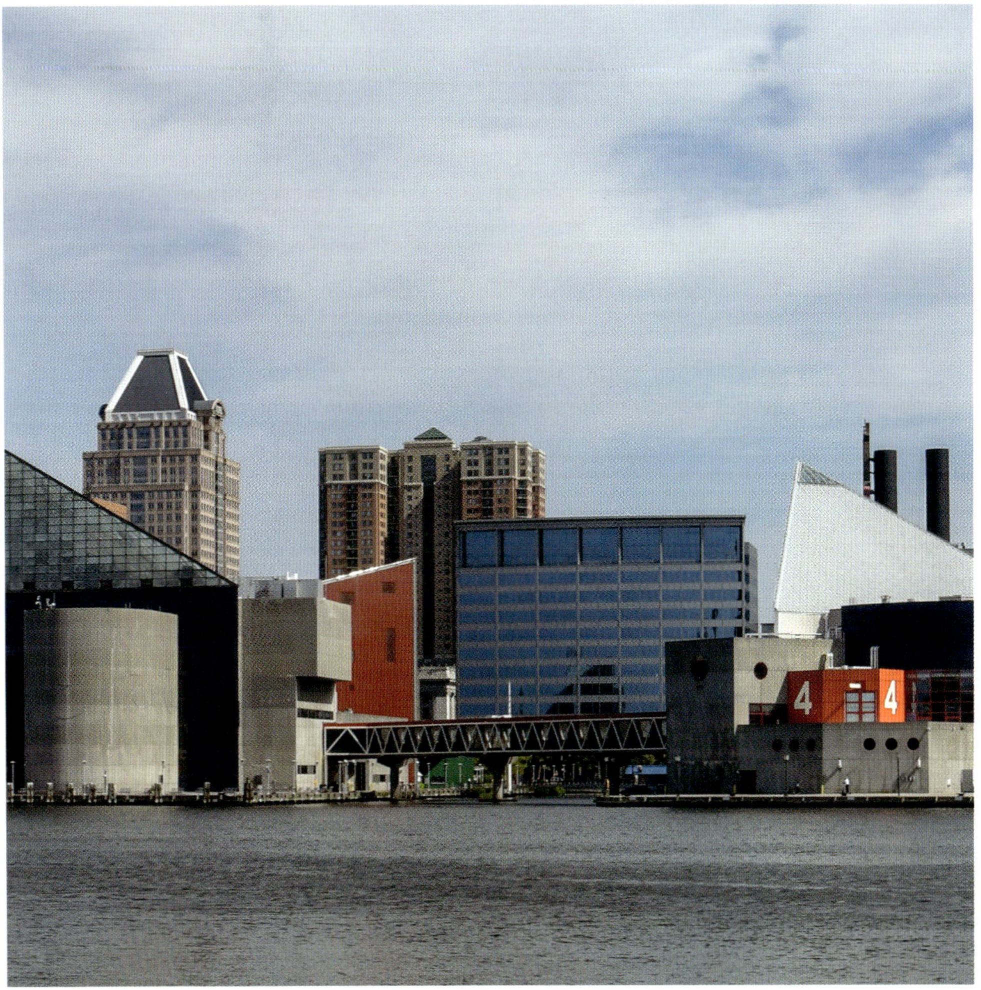

Inner Harbor

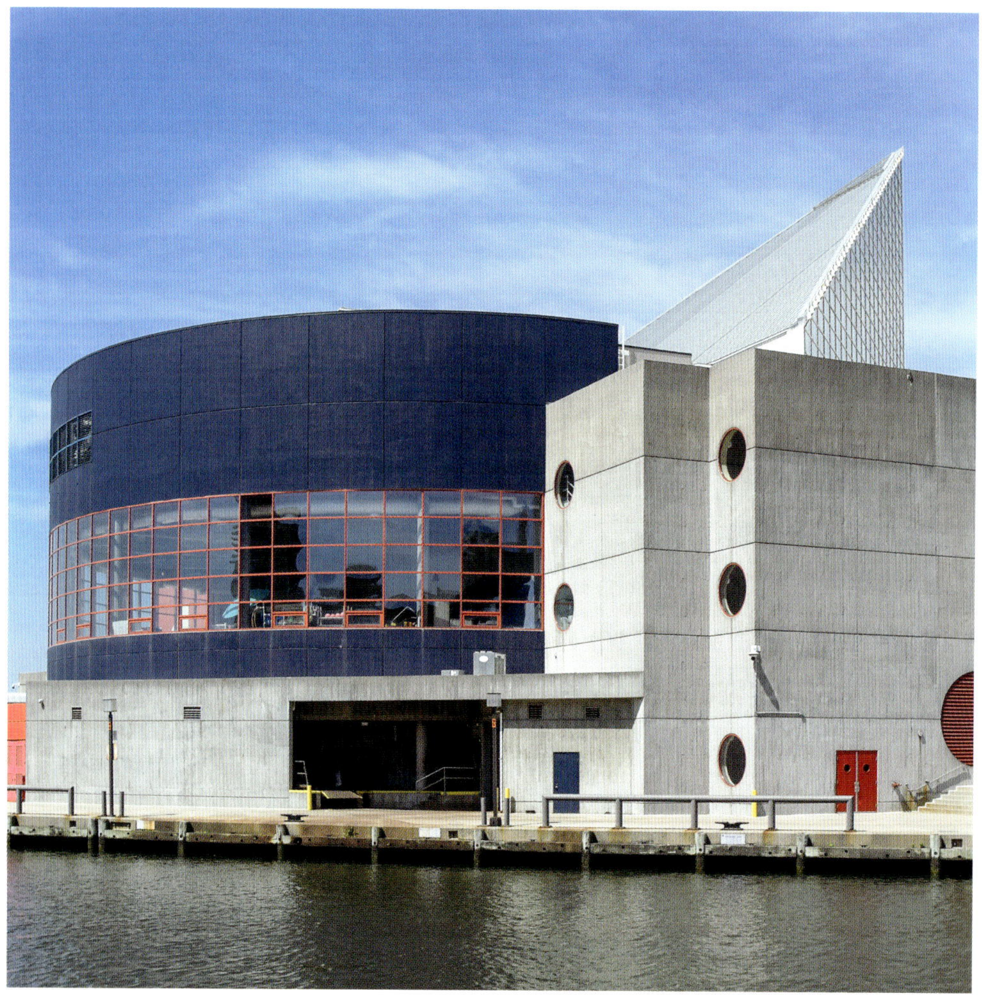

National Aquarium

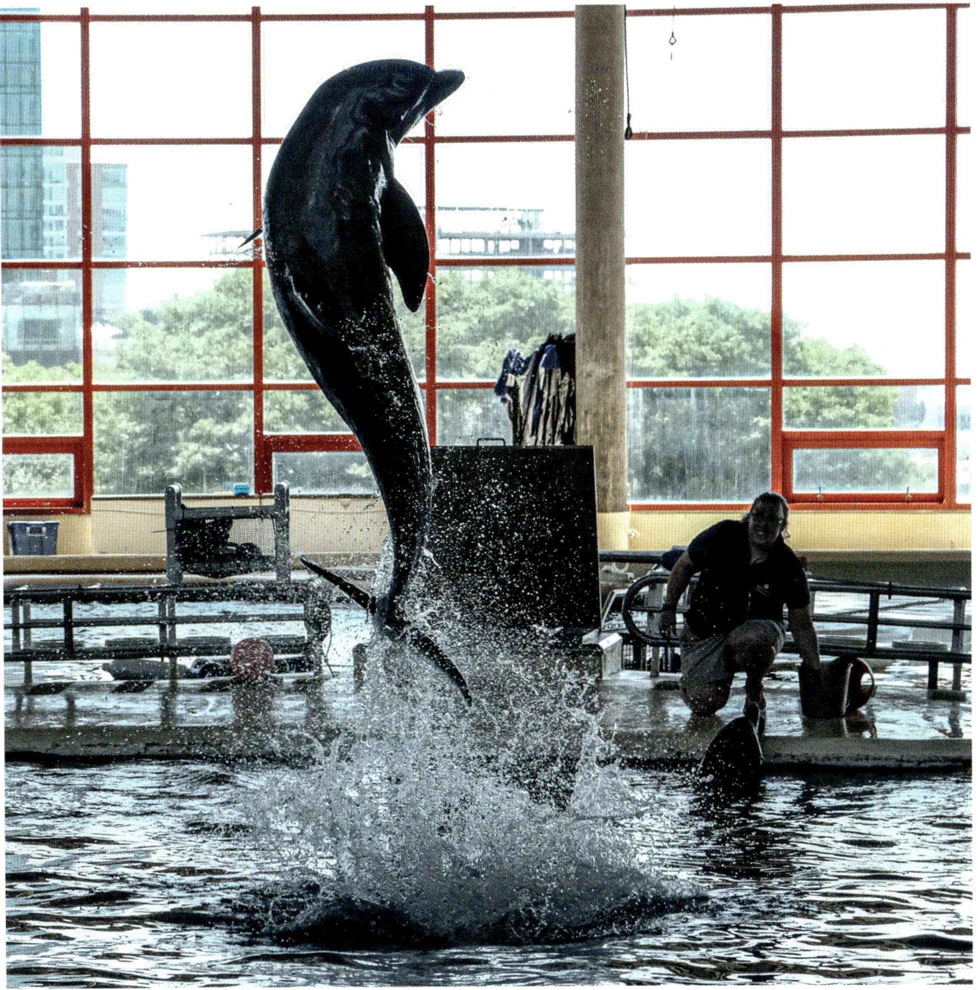

National Aquarium

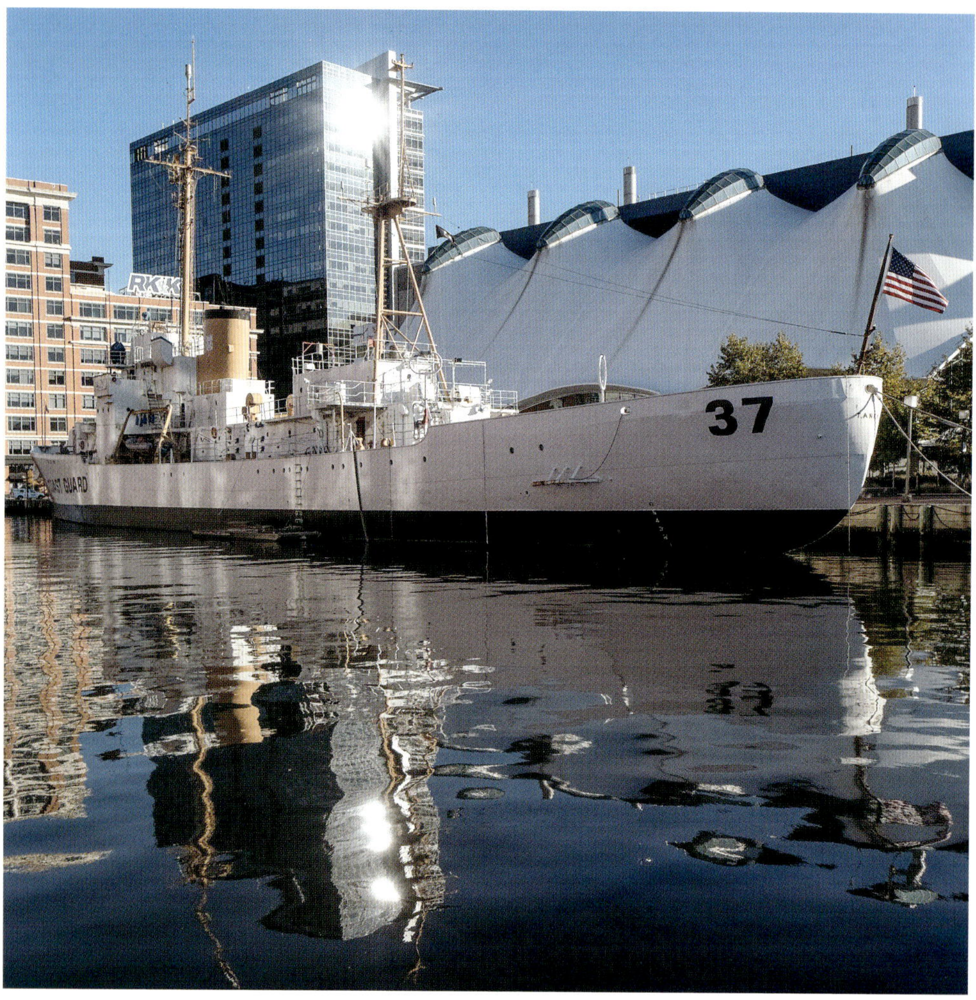

Inner Harbor

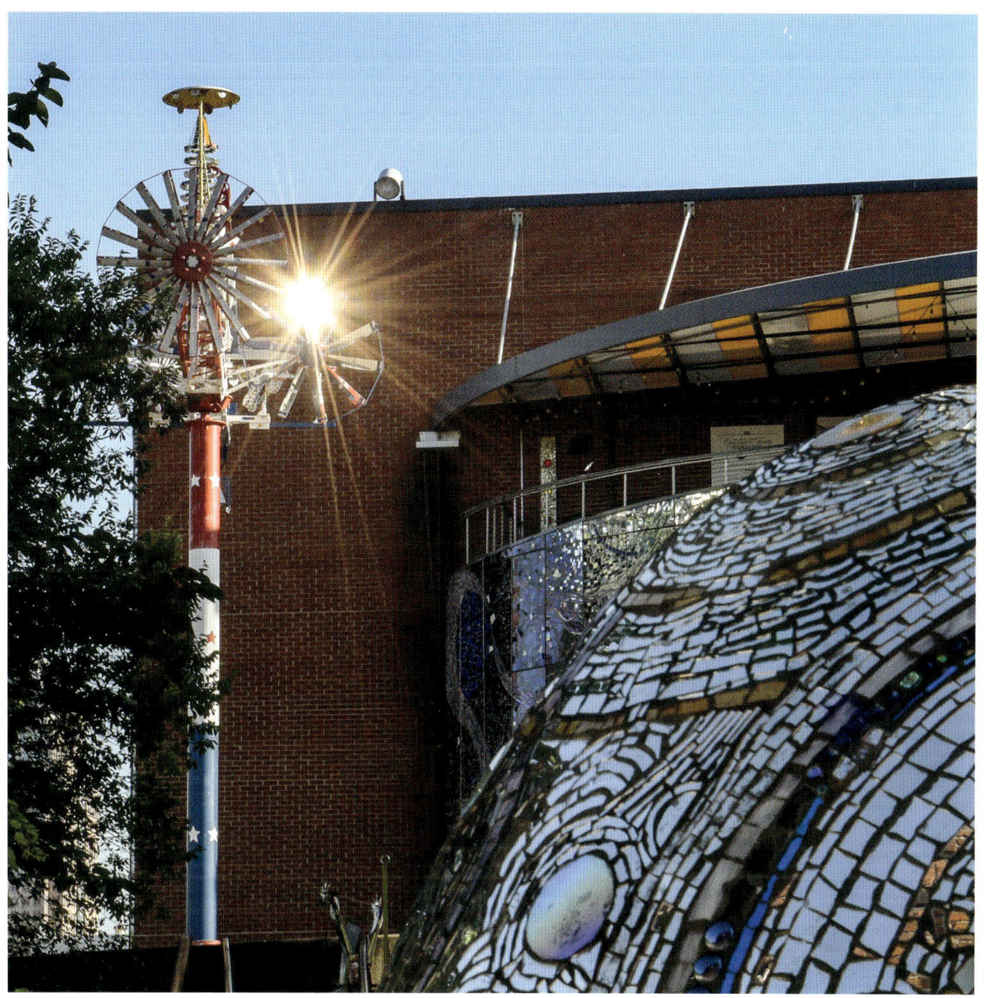

American Visionary Art Museum

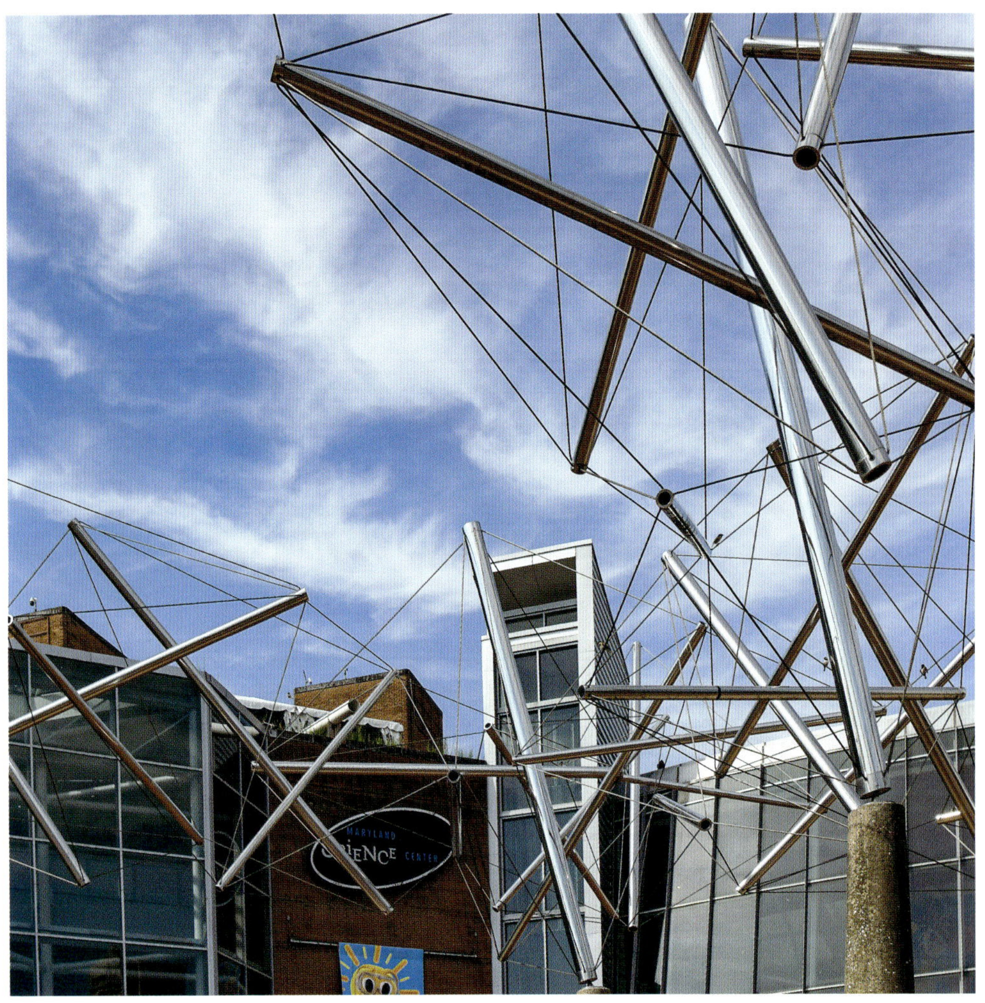

Maryland Science Center

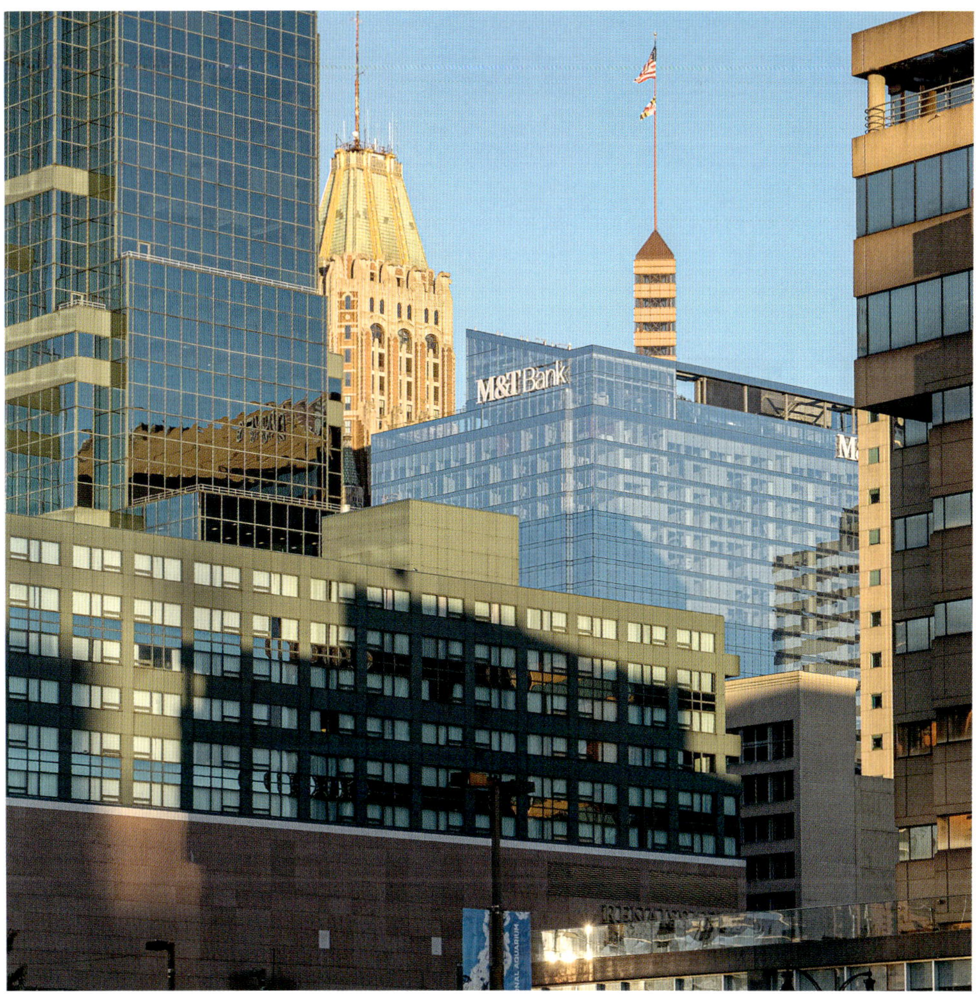

Downtown business district

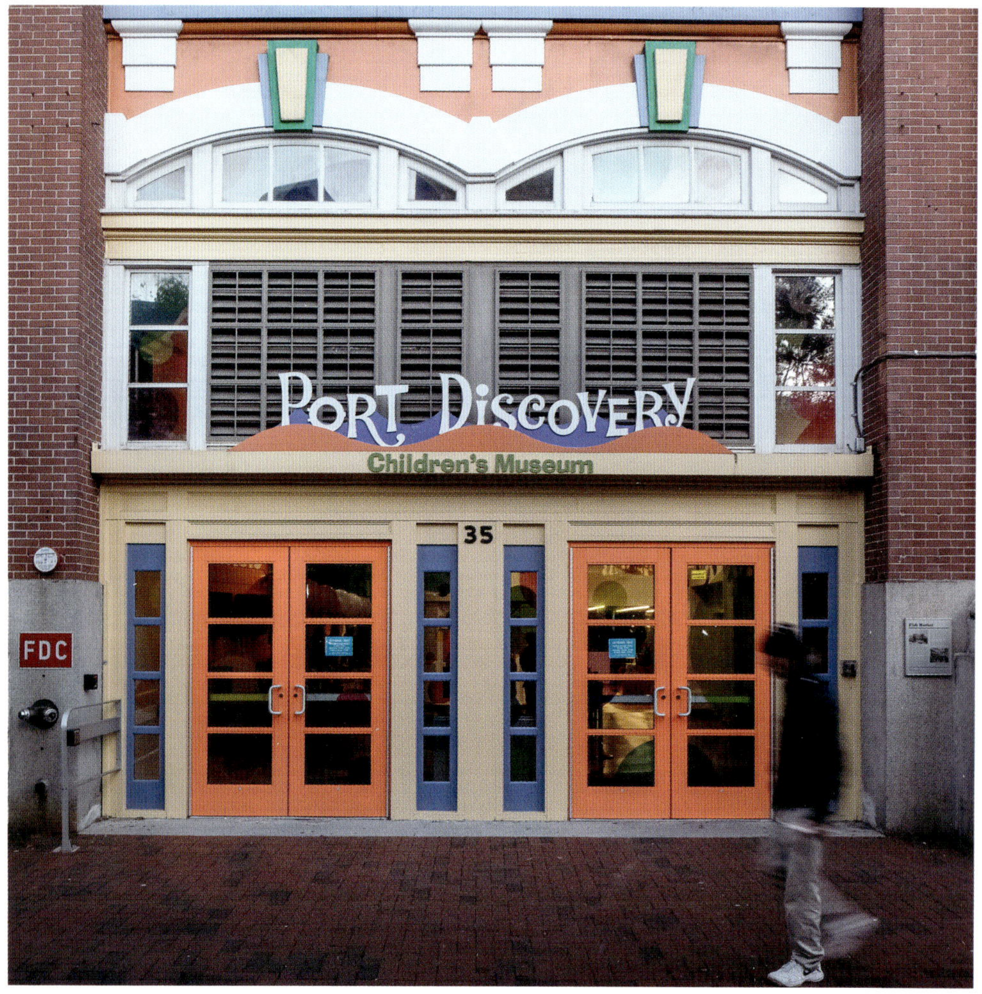

Port Discovery Children's Museum

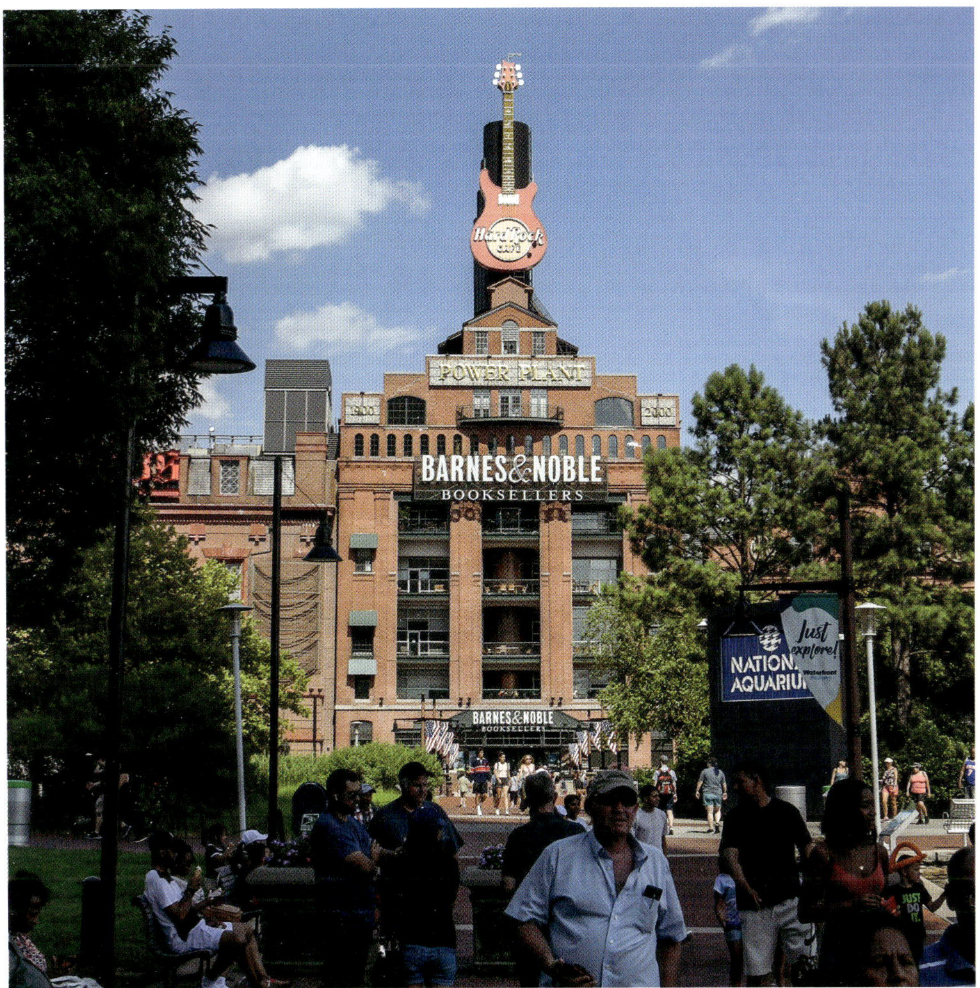

Power plant, Inner Harbor

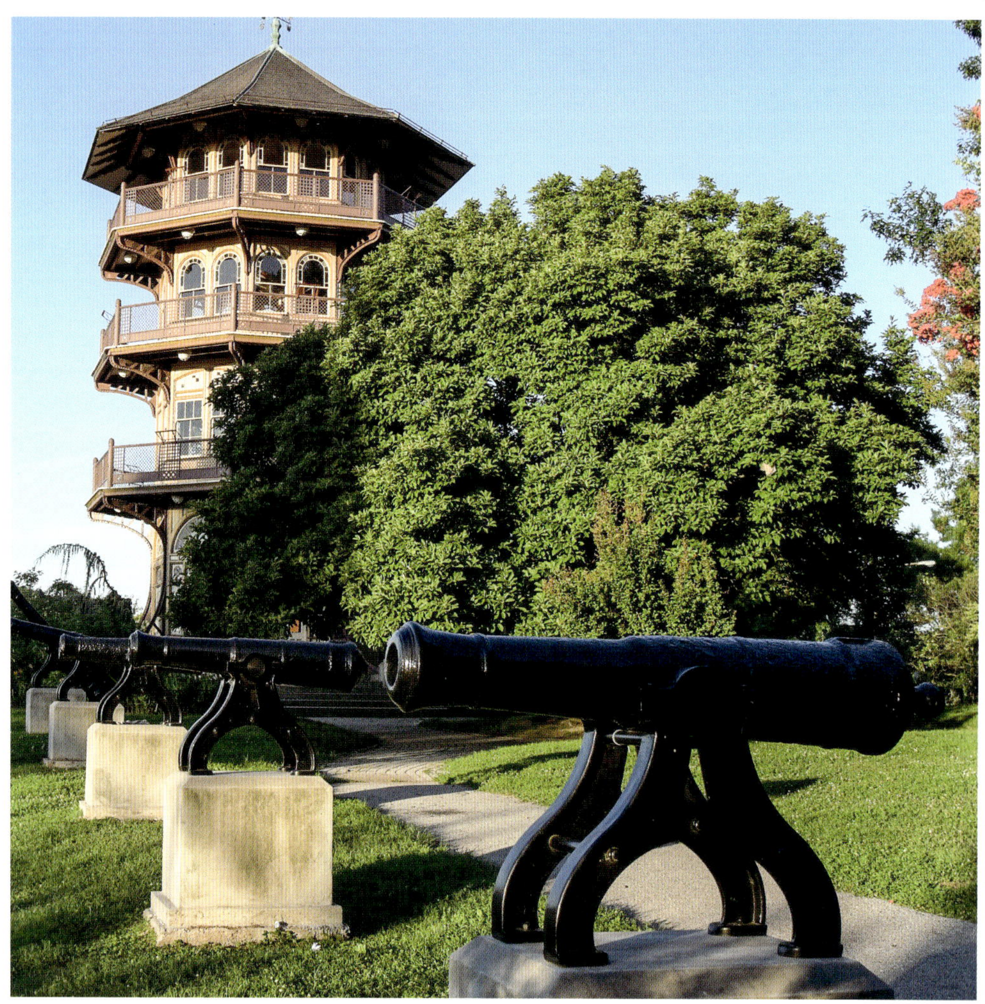

Pagoda, Patterson Park

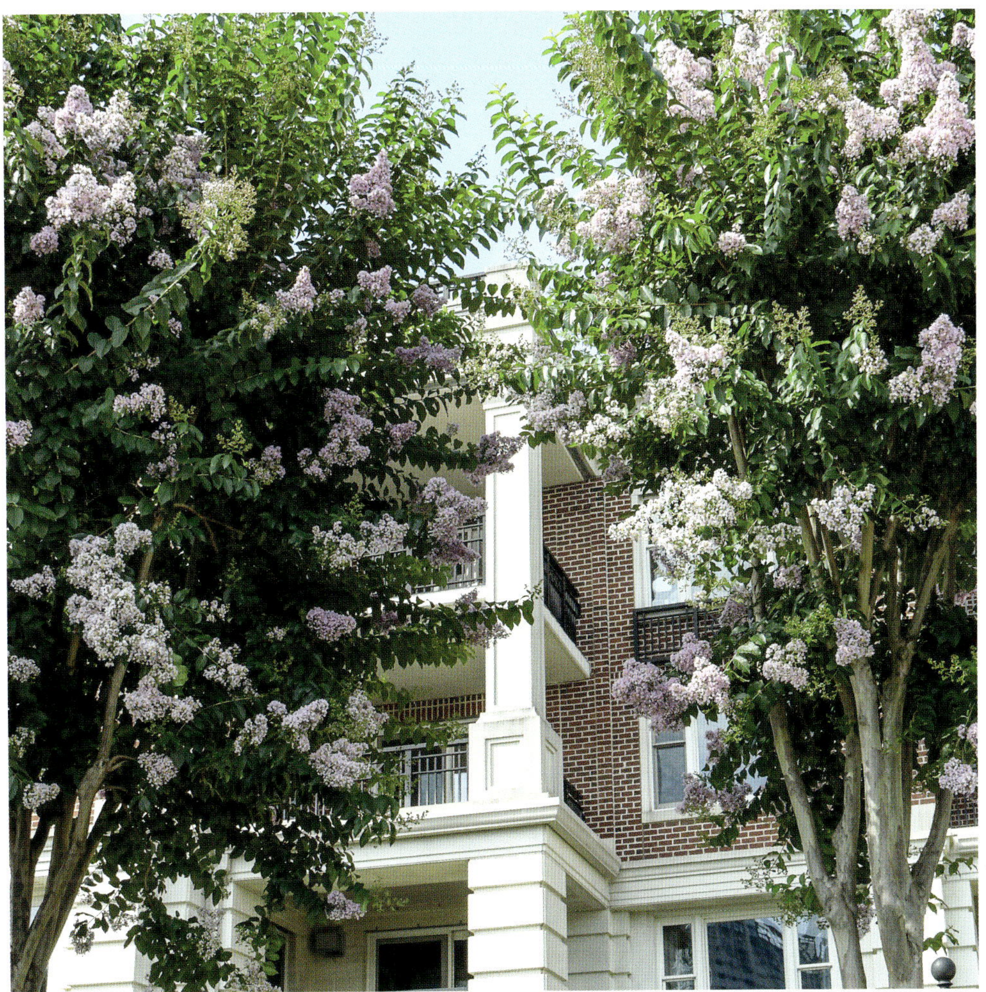

Ritz-Carlton Residences, Inner Harbor

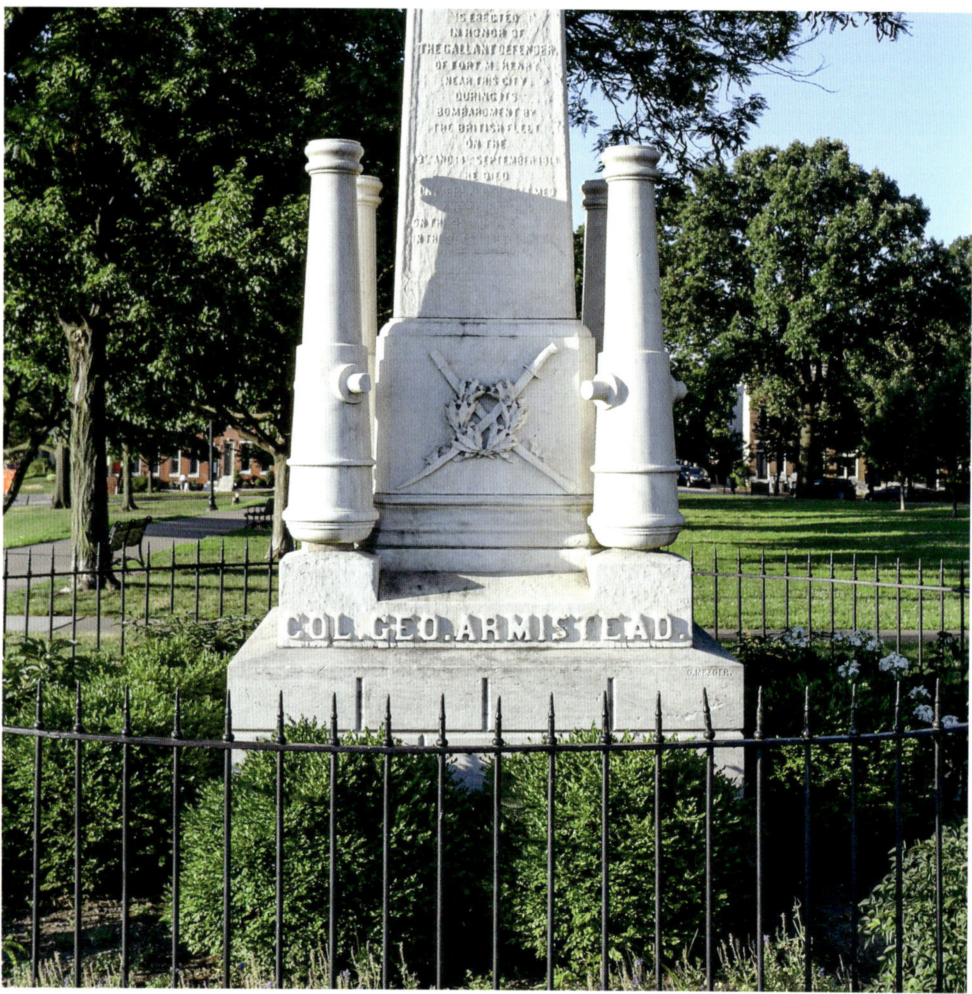

Federal Hill

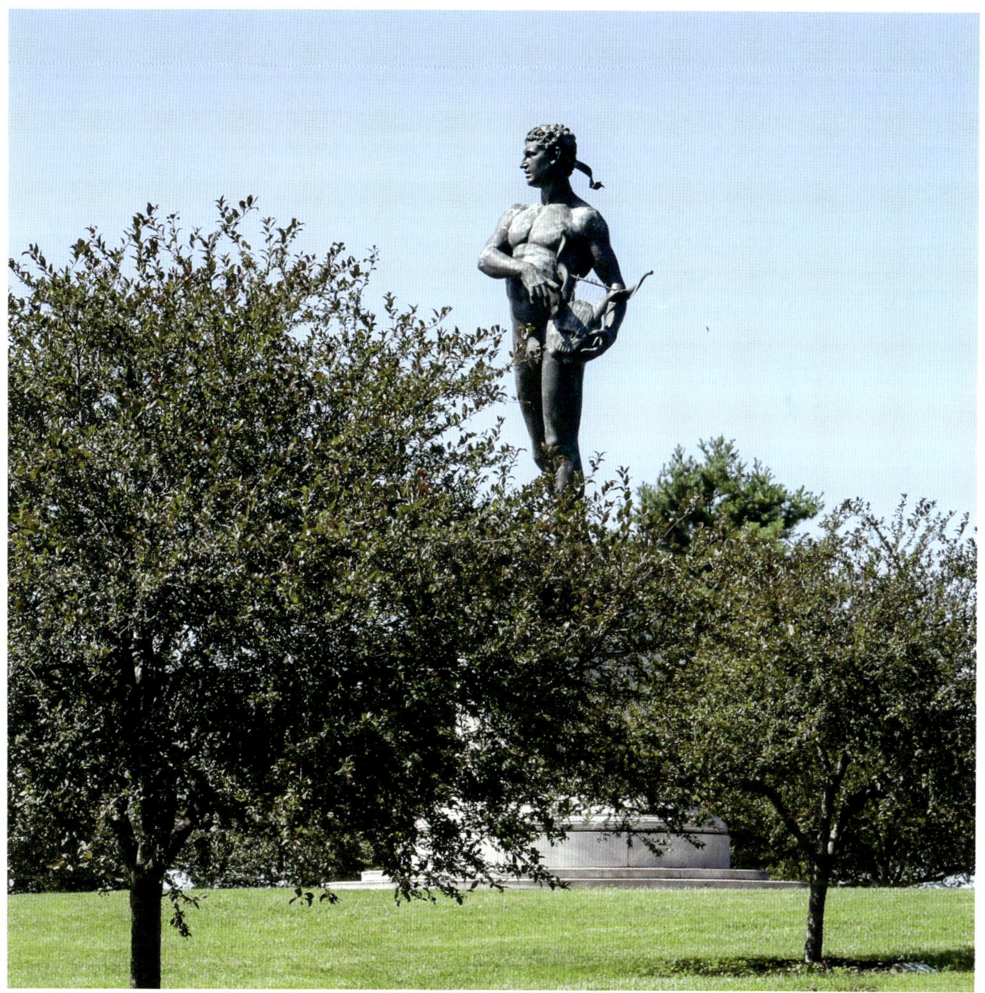

Orpheus, Fort McHenry National Monument

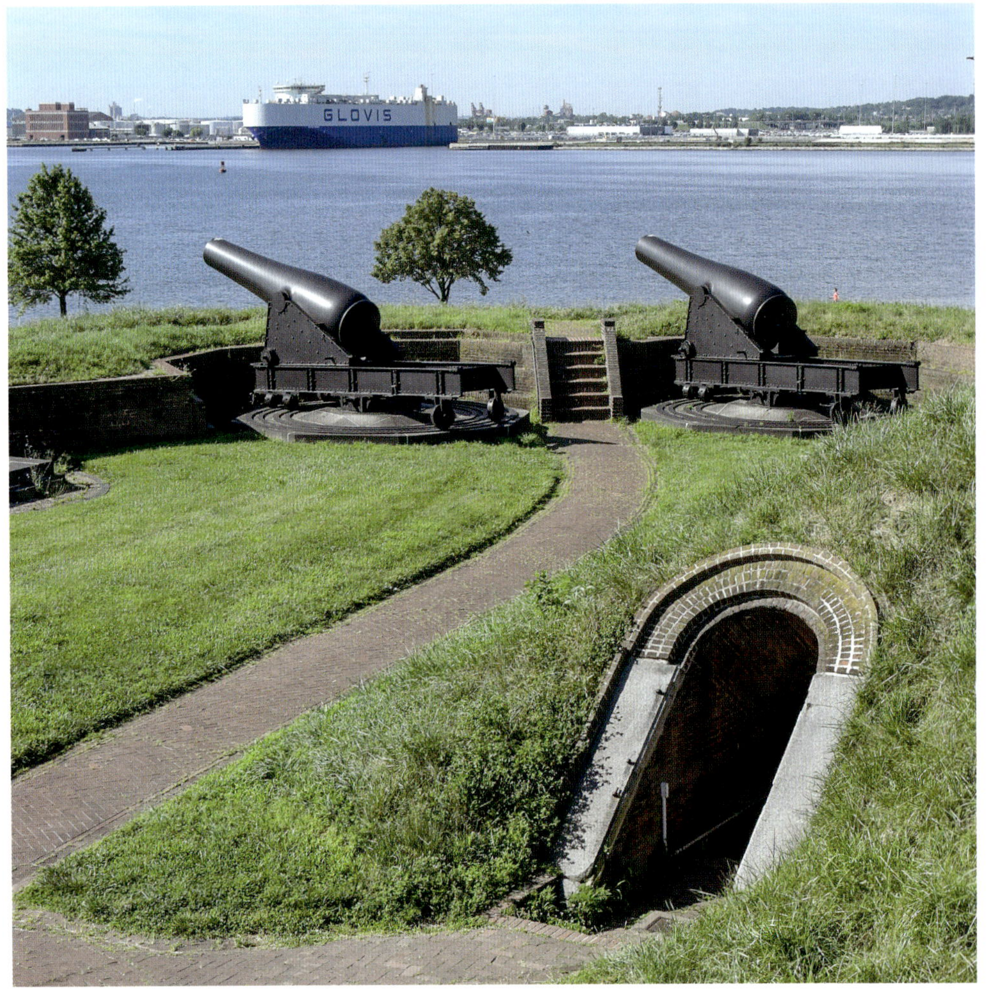

Fort McHenry

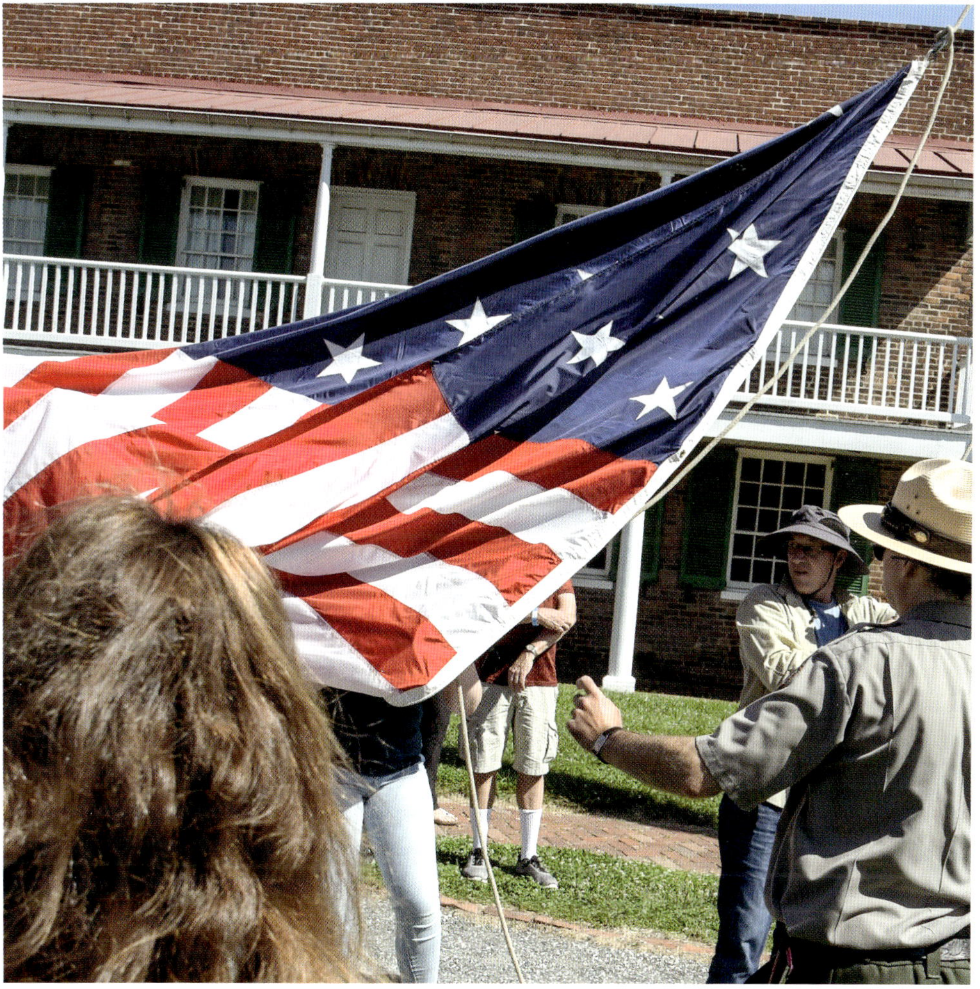

Fort McHenry

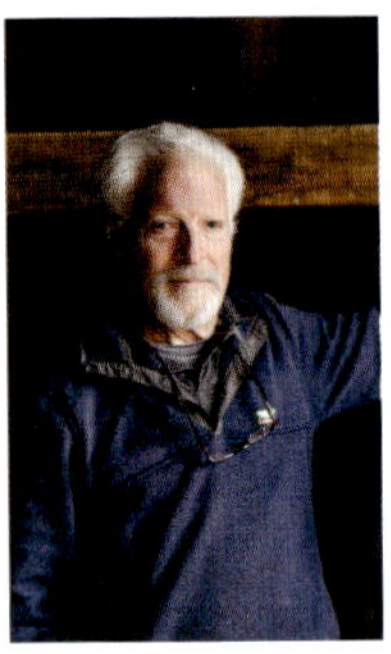

Antelo Devereux Jr. has been making photographs since he was given a Kodak Duaflex II box camera at age 10. Thus began a hobby that has grown increasingly serious as time has gone by. He is a graduate of Harvard University and has taken several courses at the Maine Media Center; exhibited in Maine, Vermont, Pennsylvania, and Delaware; and published 10 photography books. He spends his time in Pennsylvania and Maine with his family.

Other Schiffer Books by the Author:
Coastal Maine, ISBN 978-0-7643-5575-2
Brandywine Valley, ISBN 978-0-7643-5574-5
The Jersey Shore, ISBN 978-0-7643-5576-9

Other Schiffer Books on Related Subjects:
Annapolis, Jennifer B. Bodine, ISBN 978-0-7643-6064-0
The Patapsco: Baltimore's River of History, 2nd Edition, Paul J. Travers, ISBN 978-0-8703-3644-7

Library of Congress Control Number: 2021942841

Designed by Chris Bower
Type set in Bell MT/Cambria

ISBN: 978-0-7643-6359-7
Printed in India

Published by Schiffer Publishing, Ltd.
4880 Lower Valley Road
Atglen, PA 19310
Phone: (610) 593-1777; Fax: (610) 593-2002
Email: Info@schifferbooks.com
Web: www.schifferbooks.com